HERBS, HEALTH AND HAPPINESS

HERBS
HEALTH AND HAPPINESS

A Practical Guide and
Spiritual Journey

Judith Lechman

A LION BOOK
Oxford · Batavia · Sydney

Published by
Lion Publishing Corporation
1705 Hubbard Avenue, Batavia, Illinois 60510, USA
ISBN 0 7459 1883 2

First edition 1991

Printed and bound in the United States of America

Library of Congress Cataloging-in-Publication Data

Lechman, Judith C.
Herbs, health, and happiness: a practicaL guide and spiritual journey
/ Judith Lechman. – 1st ed.
ISBN 0-7459-1883-2
1. Herbs. 2. Herb gardening. 3. Herbs–religious aspects–Christianity.
4. Herbs–Utilization. I. Title.
SB351.H5L38 1991   635'.7–dc20   90–20477 CIP

Contents

Introduction

Herb gardening, at first glance, appears an unlikely vehicle for spiritual growth. Granted, other disciplines, such as fasting, meditating and journal keeping, are more mainstream approaches to developing spiritual awareness. Yet herb gardening is firmly grounded in religious tradition.

People in biblical times honored the directive to eat well to preserve the gift of life. They cultivated herbs for flavoring, scent and medicinal purposes. In a land of scanty resources, herbs both preserved and improved the taste of foods, helped heal the ill, and were critical in making dyes, disinfectants, cosmetics and perfumes.

Hippocrates, the father of medicine, taught his students the value of herbs in curing disease. His teachings formed the basis of herbal medicine practiced by Christian religious orders in medieval Europe.

By the end of the Middle Ages, monasteries were the acknowledged centers of learning and medicine. Not surprisingly, cultivating herb gardens became a formal spiritual procedure, or discipline, for those seeking to journey on the pathway to discovering God and wholeness.

Although the popularity of herb gardening has waxed and waned over the centuries, its role in the spiritual life has changed little. Herb gardening continues to provide an unusually practical method of bringing focus to our lives throughout the year. Combining exercises that are physical, social and emotional, herb gardening helps us experience God and creation from a new and richly rewarding perspective.

This month-by-month guide, like herb gardening itself, grows out of the powerful connections between body, mind and spirit. In teaching the preparation, planting and harvesting of herbs, it also demonstrates how we can cultivate an even greater transformation within ourselves and in our relationships with others.

From January to December, this guide describes how the care, uses and joys of herbs can produce a harvest of love from our hands, our hearts and our lives. If we make it part of our daily activities, herb gardening can help to infuse us with a deeper understanding of God, ourselves and the world we share.

COMMON NAMES:
Lemon balm, bee balm and sweet balm

BOTANICAL NAME: *Melissa officinalis*

ORIGIN: Middle East and Asia

Lemon Balm

The Peaceful Herb

Lemon balm has a delightful fragrance that makes this easy-to-grow perennial instantly recognizable. Gently rub its leaves between your fingers and its distinctive lemon scent will fill the air. Humans aren't the only ones who enjoy the gifts of this lovely herb. Honeybees swarm to lemon balm and are calmed by drinking its nectar. In fact, after observing their behavior, the great botanist Linnaeus used the Greek word for bee—Melissa—to classify the plant scientifically.

Lemon balm has an upright, four-sided stem referred to as quadrangular. Growing opposite one another on the stem, its leaves are heavily veined, light green and nettle-like. Pale flowers appear in July and August in tight clusters. Rather small and insignificant, they range in color from light yellow to blue-white. A mature lemon balm plant can grow as high as three feet and as wide as eighteen inches (90 x 46 cm).

Is there no balm in Gilead? Is there no physician there? Why then is there no healing for the wound of my people?

Jeremiah 8:22

Some of the earliest written references to lemon balm appear in the Old Testament. Twice the prophet Jeremiah used the fragrant balm plant as a symbol of spiritual healing. His words reflect what was common knowledge in biblical times: when applied to a wound, crushed balm leaves fight infection and keep it from spreading.

Other popular uses of lemon balm down the centuries include lemon balm cleansing lotion, said to prevent wrinkles, and lemon balm tea to relieve fever, nausea and toothaches. Melissa tea still is well known in France as a tonic for listlessness and a remedy for migraine.

Although some extravagant claims have been made in lemon balm's name, the medieval sisters in the Carmelite Order felt confident enough about the plant's medicinal properties to label the tincture of lemon balm they made "Carmelite Water." Combining lemon balm, lemon peel, nutmeg and angelica root, their tincture was considered most effective in treating insomnia, headaches and other symptoms of stress.

Today we are discovering anew that caffeine-free lemon balm tea does indeed calm the digestive tract, relax head and neck muscles tightened by tension, and soothe migraine pain. It has even been bottled as an anti-wrinkle cream. Whether it's growing on the kitchen windowsill or simmering in a teapot on the stove, lemon balm creates a feeling of well-being in the gardener.

Work for Our Hands

Lemon Balm Planting, Care and Upkeep

Lemon balm is an ideal herb to experiment with in January since it grows so easily from seed in a window box or container. A word of warning here: the seeds take a long time to germinate and must be kept at a fairly warm temperature, between seventy and eighty-five degrees Fahrenheit (21-29 degrees centigrade).

Although it will tolerate some shade, lemon balm loves rich, moist soil and full sun. As with most herbs, the richer the soil, the stronger the scent of the leaves. However, fertilizer should be worked into the soil before planting, not during the herb's growing season.

Since the roots will spread rapidly, allow plenty of space for each plant in your indoor containers. Once the seedlings reach a height of four inches (10 cm), the plants need to be thinned to six to eight inches (15-20 cm) apart. At this stage, lemon balm grows quickly, so don't be timid about cutting the plants back to keep them compact.

In early spring, you may want to take a root division, or branch of the root system, and plant it outdoors. Lemon balm can also be grown from cuttings anytime of the year.

Lemon balm has two surprising characteristics noticed by the first-time herb gardener. It will self-sow and it's a deciduous perennial, which means that the top growth will freeze with the first frost, but the plant will renew itself each spring from the roots.

After the flower clusters appear, you can cut the plant to promote more growth and begin harvesting the leaves. Fresh sprigs of lemon balm should be used immediately. If they are not, strip the leaves from the stem and let them dry in a warm shady area, preferably on a flat screen where air can circulate. The dried leaves then are ready to be stored away in a cool, dark place.

Harvesting this herb is always a delight since it leaves a lemon scent on your hands and skin that lasts long after your work is finished.

Work for Our Hearts

Creating Peace Within

It's a curious fact that following Christmas, the season celebrating the Prince of Peace's birth, we find little comfort in our daily lives. At the beginning of each calendar year, spirits ebb. January is the month most closely associated with illness, depression and suicide.

It is as though the darkness that envelopes the northern climates enters our minds and hearts. A dreary restlessness taunts us and we, like the prophet Jeremiah, wonder if there is no balm to soothe our anxious spirits.

Fragrant lemon balm offers us a timely lesson during the dark midwinter season of the soul. Capable of flourishing while confined indoors, this herb teaches us that comfort and healing know no limits. We can experience inward healing and peace if we are willing to practice the discipline needed to gain it.

Peace is a prize of the spirit, not a gift. It is available to everybody, no matter the circumstances of his or her life. But we must be willing to work for and toward it.

Like the lemon balm raised from seed indoors, peace does not happen in our spirits overnight. We have to prepare ourselves properly, practice patience and make the conditions right for its growth.

Peace doesn't flourish in doubt and fear. True peace is the peace which Christ gives. It is rooted firmly in the secure knowledge that we are not alone—that whatever difficulties we may face, Christ stands ready to pick us up, love and forgive us. Peace grows best when we allow hope and belief in God to penetrate even our darkest moments.

I am leaving you with a gift—peace of mind and heart! And the peace I give isn't fragile like the peace the world gives. So don't be troubled or afraid.

John 14:27

Lemon balm provides yet another spiritual lesson— this time in how we choose to use it. We can simply let it decorate our lives, or we can create a powerful healing force with it. So too with inward peace. We can simply act calm, or we can carry our inner, God-given peace into all our relationships.

A truly peaceful spirit, secure in the knowledge of Christ's everlasting care, has the power to erase contention, resolve longstanding conflict and ease tensions. Inward peace of this kind spreads rapidly and, nurtured by prayer, can undergird all our thoughts and actions. "Live in peace yourself," said Thomas à Kempis, "and then you can bring peace to others."

Stop all your doubting thoughts; let them buzz in your imagination like bees in a hive: if you excite them, they will grow angry and will do you much harm; if you let them alone without touching them, you will suffer from nothing but buzzing and fear. Accustom yourself to remain in peace in the depths of your heart, in spite of your restless imagination.

François Fénelon

Work for Our Lives

Peaceful Lessons

To start an indoor lemon balm garden, you need to make certain your pots are clean and the soil sterilized. Preparation remains the key to both successful herb gardening and spiritual growth.

A visual inspection for vermin, insect eggs, bacteria and fungus isn't enough. Thorough cleaning and sterilizing are needed—yet this work seems, at first, tedious and time-consuming with none of the benefits and rewards herb gardening usually offers.

You'll soon discover that your attitude makes a huge difference in how you approach and what you gain from this chore. Viewed as a nuisance, it will become just that. But seen as a way to prepare your heart as well as your indoor garden, cleaning and sterilizing becomes a time for reflection on several levels:

How will I utilize these pots?

◇ What "balm" do I need in my life right now?

◇ Where is peace absent? Where is it present?

◇ Do I nurture an attitude of calmness at work and at home?

◇ Do I accept the chaos that cannot be changed and then deal with what I can change?

◇ Am I sowing seeds of conflict or seeds of peace in my relationships?

◇ Do I look to God for true peace?

Exercise 1: Preparing to Garden

1. Soak the pots in a tub full of boiling water to which you've added liquid bleach.

2. When the water begins to cool, use a scrub brush to scour the pots.

3. Rinse each pot with hot water and let it air dry.

4. Spread the soil an inch or so deep in an ovenproof container. An old, shallow metal baking pan works well.

5. Place soil in a preheated 200-degree Fahrenheit (90-degree centigrade) oven for approximately three hours.

Make certain that no one will be around the house since the aroma is definitely disagreeable.

There's wisdom in the old Shaker saying, "Hands to work and hearts to God." Getting the pots and soil ready teaches us one way to live that axiom. Learning to brew a cup of delicious lemon balm tea is a second, more enjoyable approach.

Exercise 2: Preparing Ourselves

1. Rinse a non-metallic teapot with hot water to heat it.

2. Place two lemon balm leaves per cup of boiling water in a tea strainer.

3. Pour boiling water into the pot and let the leaves in the strainer steep in the covered pot for about ten minutes.

4. Pour the tea, add honey if you wish, sit back, sip, savor and reflect.

Try making your tea, like your spiritual considerations, an accurate reflection of yourself. Endless variations on basic lemon tea exist, so don't shy away from experimenting with tea blends, commonly called *tisanes*. One of my favorite lemon balm tisanes combines equal parts lemon balm, camomile and peppermint leaves with a generous sprinkling of dried orange peel.

As these two simple exercises show, lemon balm can enrich our lives daily if we are not afraid to practice and prepare.

COMMON NAME:
Rosemary, polar plant, compass weed

BOTANICAL NAME: *Rosmarinus officinalis*

ORIGIN: South Europe and Asia Minor

Rosemary

The Faithful Herb

When working with herbs, the novice and expert gardener alike can identify the rosemary bush immediately by its telltale sweet, pine scent. Rosemary numbers among those herbs that are as handsome in the garden as they are useful in the kitchen and bath.

An evergreen shrub, rosemary received its name from its affinity for growing by the sea. Ros comes from the Latin for "dew," and marinus means "of the sea." A native of the Mediterranean coast, it grows wild on the rocky hillsides, and when rosemary is in bloom, its silvery-blue flowers reflect the color of the Mediterranean Sea. During the harvest season, rosemary's intense fragrance can be smelled twenty miles at sea.

A tender perennial in northern climates and hardier in the south, rosemary loves moisture and misting. It requires partial to full sun outdoors and plenty of room to grow. An extraordinarily slow-starting plant, it eventually reaches a height of six feet (180 cm). Its numerous branches have an ash-colored, scaly bark on which short, narrow, tough leaves grow. These leathery leaves, which look just like pine needles, are used in cooking. Rosemary flowers bloom in April and

May, are heavily scented and are used in making cosmetics and perfumes.

There's rosemary, that's for remembrance. Pray you, love, remember.

Shakespeare, *Hamlet*

When Ophelia gives Hamlet a sprig of rosemary "for remembrance," Shakespeare's characters are speaking in a centuries-old tradition. In the language of flowers, rosemary's message has always been one of remembering the importance of friendship and fidelity.

An herb closely associated with women, its legends are legion. It is said that after the Virgin Mary dried her cloak on a rosemary bush, the flowers permanently changed from white to take on the cloak's blue color. Other legends claim that a rosemary shrub hid her from Herod's soldiers when she and Joseph were fleeing to Egypt with the baby Jesus.

Greek and Roman women would twine rosemary in their hair, believing it would strengthen their memories and quicken their minds. Anglo-Saxon brides gave their grooms rosemary on the wedding morning to guarantee that their marriages would grow in love, loyalty and wisdom. And a fifteenth-century English saying proclaimed that "where rosemary flourisheth, the women rule."

Perhaps the most outrageous legend involves an unnamed queen of Hungary who bathed in rosemary essence daily. In her seventies, she remained so beautiful that the enamored king in neighboring Poland begged her to marry him. Popularly called "Hungary Water," rosemary-scented perfume is one of the oldest-known essences still made today.

During the reign of Constantine the Great, hospital staffs burned rosemary as incense to prevent the spread of disease. Later doctors and midwives across Europe used rosemary as a disinfectant and strewing herb.

Medieval Europeans were among its greatest advocates, assuming that rosemary used as a hair rinse strengthened hair and deepened its color. Many modern, commercially prepared "natural" cosmetics rely upon rosemary for its distinctive scent and useful qualities.

Although we no longer speak in herbal messages of love and remembrance, rosemary continues to occupy a special place in the hearts of herbalists everywhere.

Work for Our Hands

Rosemary Planting, Care and Upkeep

Ironically, for an herb so well loved, rosemary can be the bane of gardeners. It doesn't adjust well to change and frequently dies even when handled with great care. In the mildest of climates, it doesn't winter outdoors well and should be brought inside to grow in containers.

Once indoors, the plant requires hours daily under fluorescent tubes, which simulate the winter sun's rays. Keeping the soil damp, without overwatering, and misting the leaves help this herb to thrive. The more skilled gardener can even shape and prune the rosemary bush in the bonsai manner, making it an attractive winter houseplant.

In early spring, once the soil is warm and fear of frost is gone, small rosemary plants nurtured indoors over the winter or purchased from a nursery can be placed in a sheltered spot outdoors. The soil need not be rich, but it must have enough lime and be able to drain well.

Rosemary cuttings, like those taken from so many other herbs, are fairly simple to cultivate. During the growing season, cut four- to six-inch-long (10-15 cm) strong stems with adequate leaf growth from the plant. Remove the lower leaves. Dip the stem first in water and then in a root-starter mixture (available from a nursery) that has vitamin additives. Then stick the cutting upright into a bedding mixture of sand and cutting compost. Although most other herb cuttings root within a month, rosemary requires much more time. If you take rosemary cuttings in early February, they will be ready to plant outdoors in early May.

A second way to propagate rosemary involves dividing the roots of a strong, fairly young plant, preferably in the early spring before the growing season. But this method holds more risks than the stem-cutting procedure.

When the rosemary plant becomes established and matures, its phenomenal growth and beauty amply reward the patient gardener. It can even weather occasional periods of intense heat and drought. Given frequent waterings and prunings, rosemary flourishes.

Its leaves can be picked any time of the year, but the aromatic oil on which rosemary's distinctive fragrance depends is most prevalent right before flowering.

Fresh leaves added to lamb, pork or chicken before roasting impart a wonderful, widely appreciated flavor. Dried or frozen in airtight containers, they lose none of their appeal. Since rosemary can overpower more delicate herbs, its use should be subtle. It should enhance, not dominate, the food it flavors.

Work for Our Hearts

Remembering Friendship and Fidelity
What better month than February to recollect the meaning of faithful friends and loving relationships? Thoughts of Valentine hearts and roses vie with lengthening days and visions of early spring. The lovely rosemary plant gently reminds us that trust and fidelity underlie all our February thoughts and dreams.

We trust that the harshness of the winter season will erupt in the joyous rebirth of spring. We believe that love transcends all other emotions and that faithfulness strengthens the ties that bind us one to another.

Epicurus stated that without confidence there can be no friendship. His observation is true of all relationships, be they with family, friends or with God.

When we take that stem cutting from the rosemary bush in February, we have every confidence that it will root, if we carefully follow the guidelines. Similarly, we know that if we treat friendships, divine as well as human, with trust and faithfulness, they too will flourish.

The English essayist William Hazlitt could have had rosemary's reputation in mind when he wrote: "To be capable of steady friendship or lasting love are the two greatest proofs not only of goodness of heart but of strength of mind."

February is the month to ponder these qualities of goodness and strength, for both are needed to maintain healthy and happy relationships. With goodness of heart, we willingly give of our time and energy. With strength of mind, we refuse to give in to the temptations that destroy rather than nurture those we love.

Rosemary, the faithful herb, can also remind us of God's great faithfulness to us. Human relationships may fail, loved ones may let us down, but God has promised to be with us and love us forever.

Understand, therefore, that the Lord your God is the faithful God who for a thousand generations keeps his promises and constantly loves those who love him and who obey his commands.

Deuteronomy 7:9

But, just as the rosemary plant can be slow to take root in the ground, we can be slow to root our trust in God.

We no longer twine rosemary in our hair or make a wedding present of it. But we should never forget its lessons. Rosemary means more than remembrance. It stands for our very human need to grow in love, loyalty and wisdom. As we nurture the rosemary bush indoors and take our February cuttings, we can update that fifteenth-century saying to read: Where rosemary flourishes, love rules and fidelity prevails.

It is true that love cannot be forced, that it cannot be made to order, that we cannot love because we ought, or even because we want. But we can bring ourselves into the presence of the lovable. We can enter into Friendship through the door of Discipleship; we can learn love through service; and the day will come to us also, when the Master's word will be true, "I call you no longer servant, but friend."

Hugh Black

Work for Our Lives

Faithful Lessons

This shortest month of the year most certainly is the time to trust in the future by turning our dreams into workable plans. A few February chores that are exercises in fidelity as well as remembrance await us:

1. Order seed catalogues from nurseries.

2. Plot on paper what size and shape your outdoor herb

gardens will be. Suggestions and sketches can be found in books at your local library.

3. Determine the kinds and quantities of herbs you will grow.

4. List which herbal gifts you will make for your family and friends from your harvest.

5. Begin to save empty spice jars, vitamin jars with stoppers, wine and vinegar bottles with corks, glass jam and jelly containers.

6. Visualize now all that you will create in the warmth of the summer. Don't be afraid to see the lushness, taste the flavorings, and smell the aromatic scents produced in your garden.

7. Finally, recognize the forthcoming bounty as the fruit of your labor and God's generosity. Take time to reflect upon this partnership that creates abundance.

Exercise 1: Sending Herbal Messages

In a Valentine's Day card place a rosemary sprig "for remembrance." Also send an herbal message by tying a rosemary sprig to the gift bows on packages for those celebrating February birthdays and anniversaries.

Exercise 2: An Unusual Herbal Present

In a less traditional gesture of friendship, present someone close to you with a jar of homemade rosemary citrus jelly this month.

Either 3/4 cup (125g) fresh rosemary sprigs OR 1/3 cup (50g) finely crushed dried rosemary leaves

2 cups (1/2 litre) unsweetened grapefruit juice

2 pieces orange peel, rather large

2 tablespoons lemon juice

3 cups (675g) sugar

1 cup (225g) honey

3 ounces (85g) liquid pectin

4 sterilized 6-ounce (170 ml) jelly jars paraffin (wax)

4 springs fresh rosemary for decoration

Place the rosemary, grapefruit juice and orange peel in a small saucepan. Bring to a boil, remove from heat, cover and let steep for twenty minutes.

Strain through cheesecloth into a large saucepan. Return to the heat and add the lemon juice, sugar and honey. Stir until the sugar is completely dissolved. Bring to boil, add the pectin, and keep at rolling boil for one more minute. Remove from heat. Skim the foam from the top of the mixture and pour the remaining mixture into jelly jars.

Heat the paraffin (wax) and cover the jelly with 1/8 inch (3 mm) layer of it. When cooled slightly, place a sprig of fresh rosemary on the top of the paraffin to decorate each jar. Cover this with another thin layer of paraffin.

Place sterilized tops on jars. From colored fabric, cut with pinking shears a circle one inch wider than the jar's circumference. Place over the top of the jar and secure with matching yarn or ribbon tied in a decorative bow. Finally, place an identifying label on the jar along with a personal note, if you wish.

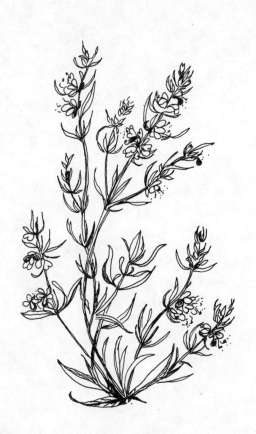

COMMON NAME: Hyssop

BOTANICAL NAME: *Hyssopus officinalis*

ORIGIN: Southern Europe

Hyssop

The Humble Herb

In a typical herb garden, hyssop is the plant most frequently overlooked. Easy to grow and care for, sweet-smelling hyssop makes a tidy low hedge or border around the garden plot. It is less well known than its more dramatic cousin, the showy lavender bush. But, given adequate attention, hyssop develops a quiet beauty all its own, flowers longer than most herbs and provides a year-round harvest.

Prospering well in either garden or pot, this herb has a marvelously tangy—if somewhat minty—taste, and it emits a heavy fragrant scent that attracts butterflies and bees. Once herb gardeners experiment with growing this unassuming plant, hyssop often becomes a permanent part of their herb collection.

Hyssop is a busy evergreen plant with square, woody stems and small, pointed green leaves that requires no special site location or treatment. For nearly six months of every year, its flowers grow in long spikes at the tops of the branches in colors that range from rose to a delicate bluish-purple. This hardy plant generally grows eighteen inches (45 cm) high and spreads out a full foot (30 cm) in width.

Surely you desire truth in the inner parts; you teach me wisdom in the inmost place. Cleanse me with hyssop, and I will be clean; wash me, and I will be whiter than snow.

Psalm 51:6–7

Hyssop was once widely cultivated for ceremonial and medicinal use. The Hebrew word for hyssop, *ezob,* means "holy plant," and biblical references to it are many. The authors of the Psalms referred to hyssop as a symbol of inner cleansing. Solomon alluded to its steady growth. And the Israelites used it to apply lamb's blood to doorposts during the Passover ritual. Several times in the Old Testament, hyssop played a prominent role in purification and consecration ceremonies. In the New Testament, a vinegar-soaked sponge was raised to the dying Jesus' lips on a hyssop branch.

In medieval times, nearly every monastery garden included a place for hyssop. The superstitious widely believed that hyssop had the power to ward off the evil eye and cleanse the skin of unsightly spots. In Elizabethan England, hyssop was taken as a cure for toothaches and ringing ears. Brewed in a decoction, it became a popular salve for killing head lice.

Before the era of room deodorizers and air fresheners, unpleasant odors were masked by throwing aromatic herbs on the floors of homes and public buildings. For centuries, hyssop was highly valued as one of these "strewing" herbs. Today we enjoy its pungent aroma as a fixative or base in potpourri.

Even now, hyssop has medicinal uses. A cup of hyssop tea is appreciated by those suffering from upper respiratory infections since it helps to clear congestion. Combined with sage, it makes a soothing gargle for a sore throat.

In keeping with its underrated status, hyssop does not make an immediate impression when used in the kitchen. Its flavor takes time to develop, growing stronger the longer the herb cooks. Unlike most herbs, it accommodates the foods it is cooked with, complementing both sweet and salty dishes.

Looking at a low hyssop hedge bordering the herb garden, we can easily underestimate the deep ritual significance and the more practical uses of this humble herb. Yet without it, our gardens, our harvest and our lives would be decidedly poorer.

Work for Our Hands

Hyssop Planting, Care and Upkeep

Hyssop grows best in a light, well-limed soil, yet it will tolerate most soils if the drainage is good. It likes the sun but also takes light shade, meaning three to four hours of direct sunlight each day. Once established, the plant becomes amply drought resistant.

In March, hyssop can be grown from seed. In colder climates, the seeds should be sown indoors in flats and then brought outside to their permanent beds.

Otherwise the seeds can be placed directly into the warm earth around the herb garden border.

When the plants are a few inches high, thin them so that they are two feet (60 cm) apart. Don't worry about the gaps in the hedge—as hyssop flourishes, it reseeds itself with great vigor. If you still wish to increase the number of hyssop plants during the second year, March is an ideal month to take stem cuttings or divide the mature roots.

Although a tidy plant, hyssop needs to be trimmed to make a more formal hedge. Spring is the best time for pruning.

Hyssop's greatest commercial value is as a flavoring agent in Chartreuse liqueur. The home gardener, however, generally limits the hyssop harvest to use in cooking, potpourris and tea. Since the oils in hyssop leaves are most pungent just before flowering, this herb ideally should be harvested prior to each successive blossoming from May to November.

There are few hard-and-fast rules governing herb harvesting for cooking, but it is especially important to remember that dried herbs are stronger than fresh-cut herbs. Believe it or not, a quarter of a teaspoon of dried hyssop leaves equals two teaspoons of fresh hyssop.

When stored in glass jars or pottery away from light and heat, hyssop leaves should keep their flavor for about a year.

Work for Our Hearts

Cultivating Humility

The American humorist Oliver Wendell Holmes, Sr., joked that "humility is the first of virtues—for other people." His observation was on target. We admire humility, mainly in others. It's just not a quality we rush to develop in ourselves.

We react to hyssop in the same way. We hardly notice the important role it can play. In terms of spiritual growth, humility is rarely seen as a dramatic virtue. It receives scant attention and even less praise. But much like a hyssop hedge, humility defines the borders of our lives.

Several centuries ago, the Curé d'Ars taught the novices under his care that humility was to the virtues what the chain was to the rosary. Remove the chain, and all the beads escape. Take away humility, and all the virtues disappear.

The humble person recognizes that there is nothing and no one beneath him or her. Every person, no matter how different, is our equal. Every task, no matter how menial, has value.

We need look no further than Mother Teresa to observe a person great in humility. Yet in the hustle and bustle of daily living, how easily we overlook her example. We forget to treat everyone that we meet as our brother or sister.

If we adopt a humble attitude, we can't help but

discard false notions of superiority. God created humans on the sixth day so that, according to the Talmud, we couldn't be boastful. In the order of creation, we came after the flea!

The humility the lowly hyssop teaches us appears to be a most fitting lesson to learn during early spring. As the world around us enters the season of rebirth, we see anew how all life emerges from such modest beginnings.

Free of pride and pretense, we can similarly flourish. Maturity and love enter when arrogance departs.

Abba John, an old desert monk, said: No one can build a house from the top down. Rather, you make the foundation first and then build upwards. His disciples said to him: What do you mean by that? The foundation stands for humility, the grace that makes all other virtues possible, he replied. You ought to start from there. All the commandments of God depend on this.

Vitae Patrum

Work for Our Lives

Humble Beginnings

As we prepare the seedbed of our herb gardens this month, we can make a special effort to include hyssop around its border. In doing so, we remind ourselves that even the lowliest gardening task holds spiritual rewards.

In growing herbs, the best results come from taking great care in preparing the site. It doesn't matter if we grow herbs in pots on a balcony or in a spacious garden. Whether in tubs or the open ground, all herbs need the three Ds to survive: depth, dressing and drainage.

Exercise 1: Preparing the Site

1. **Depth.** There is a fail-safe method to determine how deeply you must dig your soil: Gauge how tall the mature herb will grow and then loosen the soil to that same depth. Digging and breaking up the soil improves its texture, aerates it and lets water drain through it more easily.

2. **Dressing.** Herbs grow best in slightly alkaline soil that is a mixture of sand, chalk, clay and humus. Humus is nothing more than decomposed organic matter such as animal manure or the waste-plant material taken from a compost heap. Of all the dressings mixed in the site soil, humus remains the most important. Lime can be added to the soil to build up its calcium content, and a liquid fertilizer can be used through the growing season as plant food.

3. **Drainage**. When the site is dug to the proper depth and dressings added to improve it, one last task remains: making certain the soil is free draining. Dig a hole twenty-four to thirty inches (60-75 cm) deep at the lowest spot in your site and leave it open for a few days. If water collects in the hole, your drainage is poor and the herbs will wither from insufficient air around their roots. To correct this

problem, dig your garden site again, add more sand, and thoroughly break up any remaining clods.

Remember that no herb garden needs to be large since a surprising number of plants can fit into an amazingly small space, but make sure that space is readily accessible throughout the summer. In the past when herbs were grown and used on a daily basis, the gardener generally picked a site directly outside the kitchen door. Your site should be equally convenient.

Exercise 2: Preparing Hyssop Mustard

From such humble beginnings, a delicious hyssop mustard can be created simply by combining these ingredients:

1/2 cup (60 g) powdered mustard

2 teaspoons finely crushed dried hyssop

1 teaspoon finely crushed rosemary

1/2 teaspoon salt

1/2 teaspoon sugar

1/2 teaspoon ground garlic

3 tablespoons savory vinegar

2 tablespoons olive oil

Juice of 1/2 lemon

COMMON NAME: Peppermint

BOTANICAL NAME: *Mentha Piperita*

ORIGIN: Europe, Asia and Australia

Mint

The Hospitable Herb

Mint is one of the most widely used herbs in the world. There are several varieties of the delicate, aromatic perennial that go by the collective name of mint. The best known are peppermint and spearmint. Other well-liked mints, such as golden apple mint and orange mint, have equally distinctive flavors. The lovely aspect of mint is that you can choose to grow the scent and flavor you like best. Hardy mints are prolific and will flourish almost everywhere.

Peppermint is tall, shallow rooted and fast spreading, with square stems and leaves that usually have a purple tinge. The rich, deep-green, pointed leaves are sharply toothed. The small, lavender blossoms encircle the stem and grow up like thick, blunt spikes. The plant reaches a height of three feet and has the characteristic smell of menthol.

Woe to you, Pharisees, because you give God a tenth of your mint, rue and all other kinds of garden herbs, but you neglect justice and the love of God.

Matthew 23:23

Although one of the first herbs mentioned in ancient records, mint is among the least important. According to rabbinical literature, the plentiful mint was one of the "bitter herbs" the Israelites ate with the Passover lamb.

In the New Testament, faithful Jews had to pay tithes even on the inexpensive, abundant mint growing in their small kitchen gardens. Jesus' warning to the Pharisees focused on their lack of spiritual awareness. They chose to follow minute details of ritual law rather than show either love or justice to their neighbors.

The Greeks and Romans considered the use of mint leaves a sign of hospitality, a belief that holds true to this day in Mediterranean villages.

Strewn on the floor of public buildings, castles and cathedrals, mint plants acted as natural air fresheners for Europeans during the Middle Ages.

Since it grows profusely in so many areas, mint has been widely used to improve health. For centuries it has been made into a salve to soothe itchy skin. Its leaves and oil have other highly praised medicinal values, mainly in aiding poor digestion. Throughout the world, it has been used in folk medicine to relieve nervousness, cramps, insomnia, coughs and heartburn.

The resinous dots of oil found in the mint leaves and stems are still used as scents in perfumery and as flavoring in candy, gum, liqueurs and cough medicines. Mint's leaves produce soothing teas, zesty jellies and refreshing aromatics. Catnip, created from crushed cat mint leaves, brings out the playfulness in even the most sedentary cat.

Mint juleps, traditional English mint sauce, and Middle Eastern iced mint tea with vinegar and sugar are three popular international uses of mint in today's global village.

Work for Our Hands

Mint Planting, Care and Upkeep

The newcomer to herb gardening may find mint a delightful problem: it spreads so rapidly that given half a chance, a single plant will soon take over its corner of the garden.

One solution is to plant each mint stem outdoors in a container. A coffee can with both ends removed works nicely. An underground brick, clay or metal barrier will stop the roots from spreading as well.

The most important guideline in growing mint is to keep the plants separate from all other herbs—and even from other varieties of mint. Otherwise, they will lose their distinctive pungent flavors and scents.

Care and upkeep is reassuringly simple. Mint prefers sun but will flourish in partial shade. Although it thrives in moist soil, it can tolerate wide-ranging soil conditions.

Unlike other herbs, mint doesn't require richly fertilized soil. When planting, just remember to use root divisions and try to place them in the garden plot on a cool April morning. But again, mint roots manage to establish themselves when planted anytime during the outdoor growing season.

Monthly trimming of the plant tops helps keep all varieties of mint under control. The more mint you pick, the better the plant will grow.

To harvest, cut the top half three times during the season: in late spring, midsummer and early fall. Dry by hanging bunches upside-down in a cool, well-ventilated dark place, such as from an attic rafter.

As the fall season closes, mint can be brought, in containers, into protected indoor areas. A greenhouse, patio, lighted garage or basement are more than adequate winter homes for this lovely, prolific herb.

Work for Our Hearts

Learning Love's Language

In a charming doggerel on herbs, an anonymous seventeenth-century poet called mint "love's truest language." Like mint, love can grow profusely in the gardens of our lives. We need only provide the proper space for it to take root and flourish.

The mint family holds many lessons for tillers of the soil and spirit. Wild and unfocused, love becomes a weakened force. Clearly defined and directed, it grows invincible.

Just as the mint gives out its fragrance to anyone who approaches it, love from within us can radiate outward to touch all we meet. As the mint creates products of real service, so too can our love.

St. Francis of Assisi wrote that the love we hold in our hearts translates itself into welcoming eyes, helping hands and hospitable words. With such love, we learn to feed the hungry, clothe the needy and invite strangers into our lives.

Unlike the Pharisees busily counting their tiny mint tithes, we should seek to weave our daily activities into a gigantic tapestry of love. We begin by discarding any fearful or hostile threads. To our surprise, we discover how delightful it is to offer others a meal, a ride, overnight lodging, a warm smile, a listening ear and honest conversation.

A joyful unselfishness soon colors the fabric of our hospitality. We stop trying to impress others with who we are and what we have. Instead, we appreciate them just the way they are.

The abundant mint offers us a priceless lesson in spiritual growth. This hospitable herb reminds us to place love at the center of all our relationships.

In making room for friends and strangers alike, we do more than share our belongings, our emotions and our dreams. We are creating a safer, more caring world, one that reflects the loving Creator of the fragrant mint and all else inhabiting this planet.

Lord, make me an instrument of your peace. Where there is hatred let me sow love; where there is injury, pardon; where there is doubt, faith; where there is despair, hope; where there is darkness, light; and where there is sadness, joy.

O divine Master, grant that I may not so much seek to be consoled as to console; to be understood as to understand; to be loved as to love. For it is in giving

that we receive; in pardoning that we are pardoned;
and it is in dying that we are born to eternal life.

St. Francis of Assisi

Work for Our Lives

Creating Hospitality

What better way to prod ourselves gently into becoming more hospitable than to prepare for dinner guests using fresh cuttings of our early spring mint? We don't need to wait until the plants flower to enjoy their fragrance and texture. Mint in all varieties is the harbinger of spring.

Here are a few suggestions on how to decorate the table in our homes this April. In making these minty creations, we hope to please the eye and nose, tempt the palate and encourage the spirit of gracious hospitality.

1. Choose a container that complements your decor, and place masses of one variety of mint in it to create a fresh and natural effect. Anything from a hand-thrown pottery jug to an elegant crystal vase will look welcoming with your fresh mint bouquet in it.

2. Make tiny individual bouquets at each table setting, using fresh sprigs of mixed varieties of mint for contrast.

3. Encourage your dinner guests to use these mint bouquets for instant seasoning at the table. A sprig of fresh mint adds interest to iced beverages, fresh fruit salads and cooked peas. Chopped mint provides a nice

change from parsley as garnish on new potatoes, lamb and chicken. You may want to plan your dinner menu with specific mint uses in mind.

4. Twine fresh mint into a small wreath and use it to encircle the base of candlesticks placed at each end of the table.

5. Select sprigs of mint and twist them into napkin rings. If you don't have enough early mint to make these rings as full as you like, you can wrap mint sprigs around your favorite napkin rings. These designs can be as simple or elaborate as you wish.

Day by Day

◇ Give a welcoming smile to at least one new person a day.

◇ Once a week, go out of your way to help a neighbor or friend. Drive a shut-in to the grocery store. Babysit for a young mother, giving her the gift of a few hours to herself. Take a nephew or niece to a health club, the park, a movie—anywhere where you two may spend a few pleasurable hours together.

◇ Seize the opportunity to lend a helping hand or ear to family, friends or acquaintances when the occasion arises. You'll be surprised how often you can assist and, in turn, be assisted by everyone around you. At least once during this month of April, plan a specific occasion where you extend hospitality to one or more people. Volunteer a few hours' work at a local food bank. Visit an elderly relative in a nursing home. Invite an acquaintance to join you and other friends for dinner.

COMMON NAMES:
Tarragon, French tarragon, little dragon

BOTANICAL NAME: *Artemisia dracunculus*

ORIGIN:
Southern Europe, Caspian Sea,
Siberia and eastern United States

Tarragon

The Cherished Herb

Perhaps no other herb is so cherished by the gardener as tarragon. Consider the fact that tarragon is a rather ordinary looking herb with limited use outside the kitchen, and this love appears remarkable.

Not particularly attractive even when flowering, tarragon smells deliciously like fresh-mown grass. It is sweet yet pungent. This herb is valued almost exclusively for its distinctive aroma and the flavor it gives to foods. Dried tarragon leaves and flowering tops add tang to a wide range of culinary dishes, making it an essential herb to the sophisticated cook.

A word of warning to the beginning herbalist: Don't confuse the savory French tarragon plant with the nearly tasteless Russian variety, also known as false tarragon. Although they look almost identical, only French tarragon has the telltale piquancy that makes this herb so coveted by makers of seasoning vinegars and blends.

A slow-growing, half-hardy perennial, tarragon reaches a height of three feet (90 cm). Yet it can be trained to become a ground cover since it spreads by underground runners, called rhizomes, which develop both roots and leafy shoots. Tarragon needs full sun, good drainage and steady feeding to gain maximum fragrance. Its narrow, bright green leaves taste like licorice or anise. In contrast to the shiny leaves are the dull greenish flowers that occasionally appear. Sterile except in very warm climates, they don't open fully. But on a warm day in May, French tarragon adds interesting background color and a delicious aroma to any garden or kitchen.

Nothing makes a thing beautiful but the presence and participation of Beauty.

Plato

The Greeks were the first to write about tarragon. They admired its fierce flavor and thought tarragon tea a sure stimulant when appetite had been lost due to illness. In herb gardens throughout the Mediterranean region, tarragon was grown right by the garden door. The cook hardly needed to put a foot outside to gather this important culinary herb.

To the Arabs as well as those on the European continent, tarragon became more than a tasty seasoning or appetite stimulant. During the Middle Ages, it was used widely and effectively to fight pestilence.

It is believed that the word tarragon comes from the Arabic **tarkhum**, which means "dragon." Originally the name was given because of the herb's snakelike rhizomes and roots. By the sixteenth century, when the French were calling it **estragon**, or "little dragon," the name referred more to its ability to combat plague.

Today, tarragon is cultivated mainly for its leaves, which are used as a seasoning. Although commercial tarragon tea advertises itself as a cure for insomnia, tarragon is rarely used medicinally or in cosmetic preparations. This herb's versatility and value rest in the wonderful ways it can be used in the kitchen.

Tarragon traditionally has been the third herb used in **fines herbes** blend (along with chervil and chives). It is the main ingredient in *bearnaise*, sauce tartare and green goddess salad dressing. In addition to making an excellent herbal white wine vinegar, tarragon is a must in marinades and eggs benedict. It complements but never overwhelms poultry, seafood and roast meat dishes. Finally, fresh tarragon leaves add distinctive flavor to both salads and soups.

Work for Our Hands

Tarragon Planting, Care and Upkeep

Although native to a number of different climates, French tarragon can be difficult to establish in the garden. Two factors are critical. Tarragon plants require good drainage and a period of dormancy between growing seasons.

One paradox tarragon presents is that, although it needs a cooler climate for its dormant stage, the plant will freeze in the ground if the weather becomes too severe. Care must be taken to cut back the plant in late autumn and protect its roots with mulch before winter arrives.

Another unusual aspect of tarragon is that its seeds are sterile in temperate climates so it must be propagated by root division or stem cuttings. May is an ideal month in almost all places to divide the plants and take cuttings of rooted shoots. Always divide and cut from well-established clumps.

Nurseries worldwide stock healthy, young French tarragon plants, which you can transplant in either your garden or containers. Tarragon flourishes in pots placed outdoors during the growing season and then carried inside over the winter.

Remember that all herbs kept indoors need replacing more often than those in your garden. Even with regular feeding and care, the soil becomes more quickly exhausted.

A good rule to follow in growing French tarragon in containers is to repot tarragon in new soil every year. For strictly outdoor herbs, divide and replant in fresh soil every three to four years. Again, May is an excellent month to take care of this important task.

Tarragon thrives in an organic garden, for it has no serious pest or disease problems. To go from planting to harvest time takes about sixty days.

Pick the tender top leaves and occasional half-opened blossoms as you need them. Don't hesitate to cut back the top growth several times each season, helping the plant to become bushy and spread as ground cover. The average gardener needs no more than one healthy mature tarragon plant to supply a household's year-round need for this herb. Plant more and you'll have plenty to share with friends and family.

It is when a man begins to know the ambition of his life not simply as the choice of his own will but as the wise assignment of God's love; and to know his relations to his brethren not simply as the seeking of his soul for these souls because they all belong to the great Father-soul; it is then that life for that man begins to lift itself all over and to grow towards completion upward through all its length and breadth.

Phillip Brooks

Work for Our Hearts

Cherishing and Being Cherished

While many sing June's praises, I prefer spring's sweetest month—May. As I work in my herb garden during this magical time, Henry Wadsworth Longfellow's words are never far from my mind. I find myself agreeing anew with his assessment of May as "a perfumed word, an illuminated initial. It means youth, love, song, and all that is beautiful in life."

I feel similarly about French tarragon, an herb that comes to life each May. Although it adds no dramatic touch and offers little color, this herb is the heart and soul of a quiet yet beautiful bounty.

I cherish tarragon for more than its generous harvest. It teaches us a powerful lesson in love. No easy plant to grow, it demands an abundance of time, energy and attention. And it rewards us accordingly. The loving effort we put forth returns to us tenfold, creating a never-ending cycle of cherishing and being cherished.

A writer on Christian ethics, William Law, wrote that all we find sweet, delightful and amiable in this world is nothing else but "godly love breaking through the veil." With God's loving nature to imitate, we can't help but bring a harvest of love into our own lives.

From its serpentine roots to its fragrant leaves, tarragon provides us with abundant insights into this spiral of love.

We need to learn to cherish others as we are cherished by God.

Dear friends, let us love one another, because love comes from God. Whoever loves is a child of God and knows God. Whoever does not love does not know God, for God is love. And God showed his love for us by sending his only Son into the world, so that we might have life through him. This is what love is: it is not that we have loved God, but that he loved us and sent his Son to be the means by which our sins are forgiven. Dear friends, if this is how God loved us, then we should love one another. No one has ever seen God, but if we love one another, God lives in union with us, and his love is made perfect in us.

1 John 4:7–12

Shakespeare captures the idea of the spiraling nature of love in these three lines from **Romeo and Juliet**:

My bounty is as boundless as the sea,

My love as deep; the more I give to thee,
The more I have, for both are infinite.

Remembering God's infinite bounty of love will help to see us through the dormant seasons of the soul. Darkness and cold shouldn't deter us. Learning from the tarragon, we must trust God to bring us to warmth and light once again.

Love, much like tarragon, should have roots that spread across the face of the earth while its branches reach toward the heavens. During this month, we can establish love's roots and nourish its branches by sowing spiritual seeds, both large and small.

We can express our love for others through prayer as well as through our caring words and deeds. The closer we become to God the more able we will be to express his love in all we do and say.

In this way, we enter the sacred spiral and feel what cherishing and being cherished truly means. By bringing the infinite beauty and bounty of God into our lives, we are free to release it into the lives of all we encounter.

Work for Our Lives

Nurturing the Sacred Spiral of Love
Since the tarragon seed generally is sterile, one way to share the bounty of our herb gardens is to give a pot of tarragon to friends when dividing the roots in May. Or, when we go to the nursery to buy new tarragon, we can pick up a couple of extra plants to give as gifts during this month.

Learning to give and receive love in our lives doesn't come naturally. Like most qualities, reciprocal love takes time and practice. In nurturing our herb plants in this last full month of spring, we can learn how to nurture the sacred spiral of love.

Exercise 1: Transplanting

In late winter and early spring, we prepared the outdoor garden site and allowed the ground to settle. Now we have obtained the plants, including tarragon, that are difficult to grow from seed, and we're ready to transplant these nursery purchases into our gardens.

Following these nine basic steps can be an exacting discipline and a labor of love. Yet the rewards are almost immediate: satisfaction in a job well done and a quiet joy from being in touch with the earth and its Creator.

1. When you arrive home with your plants, place them in a sheltered area until you begin transplanting.

2. Don't let them dry out. Thoroughly soak the plants and leave overnight before putting them in the garden.

3. Choose a warm, damp morning, preferably overcast, to plant.

4. After digging a hole deep enough to hold the plant, remove the herb gently from the pot, being careful not to disturb its root ball. The younger the plant, the more careful you must be.

5. Set the plant in the hole with the soil ball beneath the ground level.

6. Fill around the plant with a combination of earth, compost and leaf mold. Pack it down well.

7. Water the plant with a light soaking mist.

8. Place an identifying label next to the plant so you won't forget the name of the herb you've planted.

9. Protect the plant by keeping it shaded from the sun and wind for the first few days until it becomes "hardened" or established.

Exercise 2: Sharing the Bounty

With this herb butter recipe, tarragon easily makes the trip from the garden to the table within weeks of planting. It's incredibly simple and makes a charming gift when packed in apothecary jars, stoneware crocks, or other unusual containers.

1. Gather together 1 cup (225 g) softened butter or margarine, 4 tablespoons fresh, chopped tarragon leaves, 1 tablespoon chopped chervil, 1 tablespoon chopped dill, 1 tablespoon chopped mint and 1 teaspoon lemon juice.

2. Pound the butter in a mortar until smooth. Add the chopped herbs and pound again. Add the lemon juice to taste. If you don't have time to pound the mixture, use a blender on high speed for one minute.

3. Pack in a covered container and chill until firm.

4. Label the container with suggested uses: "Serve with grilled steaks, fish, chicken, corn-on-the-cob or noodles."

5. This butter keeps well up to a week in the refrigerator and can be frozen for future use or gift-giving.

Whenever you are unfamiliar with the flavor of an herb, add it to a small amount of butter, margarine or cottage cheese. Let the mixture sit for an hour or so to absorb the flavor, and then try it on a plain cracker.

COMMON NAMES:
Costmary, alecost, Bible leaf, Sweet Mary,
balsam herb.

BOTANICAL NAME: *Chrysanthemum balsamita*

ORIGIN:
Mediterranean and eastern United States

Costmary

The Cheerful Herb

This pretty, leafy herb is a plant known by many names, all reflecting its unusually cheerful character. Costmary grows like a weed wherever planted, but it's a friendly spreader that looks great growing along a border or adding needed color to a quiet section of the garden. Like everything else about this plant, its fragrance is decidedly pleasant, combining mint, lemon and balsam scents. With its bright yellow flowers shaped like buttons, the costmary plant in full bloom never fails to light the herb gardener's face with a smile.

A hardy perennial, costmary is aggressive and self-sowing. Yet for all its rapid spreading, it will grow attractive foliage only in shade. When planted in full sun, it bears long, narrow, light green leaves that are highly aromatic and serrated. Clusters of yellow flowers on erect stems make their appearance in early summer and continue through early autumn. Under sunny conditions, costmary will reach a height of three feet (90 cm).

To call an object in the world sweet and lovely is

not yet to know the Sweetness that is God.

Angelus Silesius

Costmary takes its name from the Latin *costus*, an Oriental plant, and **Mary**, referring to the Virgin Mary. Several legends link costmary with Mary's sweet disposition and cheerful outlook.

In Elizabethan England and, later, in the American colonies, a popular minty drink made from costmary leaves was called Sweet Mary Tea. One of its recommended characteristics was that it didn't need to steep long to have a strong taste. Long before Sweet Mary Tea was popular, costmary had been harvested throughout central Europe for use in making ale and beer. In fact, this herb is still known in many European countries as alecost.

Perhaps its most colorful name was bestowed by early American settlers, who affectionately referred to it as Bible leaf. Before church services they placed fresh leaves in their Bibles as bookmarks, hoping they wouldn't have to serve a double purpose. If the sermons grew long and dull, they knew they could chew the costmary leaves to keep awake. In the Amish communities of central Pennsylvania, this practice continues even today.

For hundreds of years, it has been said that "costmary grows only in gardens of the righteous." In reality, this light-loving plant grows like a weed whenever and wherever possible. Its uses today are widespread as well.

Dried, costmary is a wonderful addition to potpourris and herb cushions. It continues to be useful in flavoring beer and ale. Its tansy-scented yellow flowers provide color and character to ornamental arrangements. When tender and young, its leaves can be sprinkled lightly over salads. Since its flavor is as powerful as its growth, costmary should always be used sparingly.

Work for Our Hands

Costmary Planting, Care and Upkeep

This sun-loving plant, appropriate for the long, bright days of June, is easy to start from seed. Once the ground is warm and all danger of frost is past, costmary seeds can be sown in well-drained soil. The only other precaution to take in planting is that the plants should receive at least six hours of sun each day during the growing season.

Costmary has a tendency to look "leggy" unless frequently clipped. Since it spreads rapidly by underground rhizomes, this herb needs to be divided every three years to keep it under control.

The oils in its leaves are strongest just before flowering in mid-June, making this month the best time to begin harvesting costmary. Since you don't want the plants to flower and then die in their natural cycle, monthly trimming of the branch tops is recommended from now through early autumn.

Harvesting requires some preparation. Make

certain that the flower buds have begun to form but haven't actually started to open yet. The day chosen to pick the leaves should be dry. Moisture is the enemy of a healthy harvest. If you wish to spray the plants clean before picking, be sure they've had a chance to dry off completely. Costmary, or any other herb, shouldn't be harvested when the heat of the day is on the plant. Late morning on a sunny day with low humidity is ideal. When harvesting, never pick off more than one-fifth of the total number of leaves on any plant. Otherwise, it may not survive.

In cold-weather areas, costmary dies to the ground in autumn but resprouts the following spring. If you decide to bring this herb indoors to grow over the winter, remember to keep its container on a sunny windowsill and trim the plant back monthly.

Work for Our Hearts

Seeking God's Light

From God's first words in Genesis—"Let there be light"—to the final chapter in Revelation where God promises to banish darkness, light is a powerful, recurring symbol of God and godliness in the Bible.

In June, the month with the longest daylight hours, it seems fitting to turn our attention to following the lighted pathway of spiritual growth. In contemplating the cheerful, light-seeking costmary, we realize anew how closely related goodness and good-naturedness actually are.

A few years before Christ's birth, Ovid stated that "a good disposition is a virtue in itself and it is lasting; the burden of the years cannot depress it, and love that is founded on it endures to the end."

Cheerfulness, affability, good humor, *joie de vivre*— there are many words to describe this wonderful trait. Like the costmary despite its various labels, cheerful people are instantly recognized and admired. In them, we see the inner light and worth that is one reflection of God's goodness.

During the summer months, costmary shares its abundance with everyone who enters the herb garden. Cheerfulness is much the same. As Ralph Waldo Emerson wrote, "The more it is spent, the more of it remains."

But a cheerful spirit, as with all positive traits, doesn't happen without effort. Wishing to be good-natured will not make us so. Being cheerful on the surface while unhappy deep down will soon wear thin. A marvelous Congolese proverb asks: Even though the teeth are smiling, is the heart? For our lives to help bring light to a world darkened by war and hunger, homelessness and despair we need to discover the guiding light of Jesus Christ. "Whoever follows me," says Jesus in John's Gospel, "will have the light of life and will never walk in darkness."

So as we enter sun-filled summer days, a glance at the costmary plant reminds us of God's gift of light to the world. With good cheer, we hope to spread that same light to burdened hearts and minds. Realizing that a smile is a whisper of caring, we are ready to make cheerfulness our shout of love.

Let us seek the grace of a cheerful heart, an even temper, sweetness, gentleness, and brightness of mind, as walking in His light, and by His grace. Let us pray to Him to give us the spirit of ever-abundant, ever-springing love, which overpowers and sweeps away the vexations of life by its own richness and strength, and which, above all things, unites us to Him who is the fountain and the centre of all mercy, loving-kindness, and joy.

John Henry Newman

Work for Our Lives

Spreading Cheer

Although it sounds like an easy task, spreading cheer takes discipline and hard work. Learning to affirm, uplift and encourage others runs counter to our early training and the competitiveness of Western society. Yet we can develop good-natured thoughts, words and deeds if we focus our attention and energy toward that end.

During the summer months, we generally have more daylight hours to spend with our families and friends. Drying herbs together is one way we can practice cheerfulness while preparing herbs for gifts that will spread cheer in the months to come.

Exercise 1: Drying Herbs

1. **The Traditional Approach.** Using a wooden clothes rack, hang small bunches tied upside-down and gathered together with twist-ties. Make certain that you leave enough room for air to circulate freely around each bunch. For taller herbs, such as the mints and oregano, tie together bunches with string, turn them upside-down in paper bags secured with rubber bands, and hang them from your rack. The bags should be large enough so the herbs will not touch the paper while drying.

2. **A More Modern Approach**. Set the temperature in a conventional oven no higher than 110 degrees Fahrenheit (43 degrees centigrade). If your oven registers higher than this, keep the oven door open slightly. Place the herbs in a single layer on a baking sheet and heat them until they are crisp, approximately two to four hours. The leaves should crumble easily between your fingers.

3. **A Thoroughly Modern Approach.** Place the herbs on a thick paper towel in your microwave oven and cover with a second towel. Turn on medium setting for two to three minutes. If not fully free of moisture, turn the oven on for thirty-second intervals not to exceed two additional minutes.

It helps to keep a record of which process works best with which herbs, eliminating the trial-and-error approach to herb drying.

Exercise 2: Making Sachets

Sachet-making has an old fashioned ring to it. Yet these wonderful herb presents are as popular today as at any time in the past. Sachets simply are nature's air fresheners, little pouches of crushed dried herbs used to scent clothing, closets, drawers and stationery. The major difference between potpourris and sachets is that the mixture for sachets is ground finer than for potpourris.

The basic formula for all scents combines one quart (one litre) of finely crushed herbs and flowers to two tablespoons each of spices and fixative. Here's one of my favorite classic summer sachets:

1/2 cup finely crushed dried costmary

1/2 cup finely crushed dried mint

1/2 cup finely crushed dried thyme

1/2 cup finely crushed dried rose petals

2 tablespoons dried orange peel

1 teaspoon crushed orris root, a fixative available at most florists and nurseries

For gift-giving, this mixture can be placed in colorful fabric bags stitched with flower shapes or in delicate handkerchiefs that are tied tightly with an elastic band covered by a decorative ribbon. Another suggestion is to purchase teabag papers from a health-food store, pour the sachet mixture into them and seal them shut with a warm iron. These are perfect to add to greeting cards or letters.

Sachet scents and shapes are limited only by your imagination and creativity. These are inexpensive, fun gifts that even children can make with a little help and direction. And they bring real pleasure to those who receive them.

COMMON NAME:
European angelica, garden angelica, angelica

BOTANICAL NAME: *Angelica archangelica*

ORIGIN: Eurasia

Angelica

The Adaptable Herb

Angelica is a sweetly scented, stately herb that makes a striking addition to any herb garden. This handsome plant is a giant relative of parsley and far more spectacular. Its creamy flowers mass in umbrella-shaped clusters, giving the plant a deceptively tropical look. Yet angelica can thrive almost anywhere and has adapted as far north as the Arctic Circle. Well-suited to its lovely name, angelica belongs to the rare group of herbs for which good use has been found for every part of the plant. From its edible roots to its colorful flowers, nothing goes to waste with angelica.

Technically, angelica is a biennial herb that has foliage its first year and flowers the second. When grown in partial shade and moist, rich soil, angelica easily reaches more than six feet (180 cm) in height and three feet (90 cm) in width during its second year. Yet, if you cut back flower heads before they form, the plant will have two or more additional years of growth before dying.

This herb has stout, hollow stems that are purple at the base, dark green leaves over two feet (60 cm) long, and finely toothed leaflets arranged in groups of three.

Due to its size, angelica makes a good background herb along a fence or to the rear of the garden. Its floral display in its second year usually lasts from May to early autumn.

Weep not that the world changes—
did it keep
A stable, changeless state,
'twere cause indeed to weep.

William Cullen Bryant

As its name implies, angelica has been tied to religious lore over the centuries. A guardian angel supposedly presented this herb to humans as a cure for plague. Another legend claims that angelica only blooms each year on the feast day of the Archangel Michael, giving it its name.

During the Middle Ages, Europeans chewed angelica roots to protect against evil and witchcraft. Ancient and modern herbalists alike have considered angelica both a tonic and stimulant and have used its leaves and stems to alleviate sunburn, tension, indigestion and sore throat.

In the Faeroe Islands and Iceland, angelica has always grown abundantly and is harvested as a popular vegetable. Boiled, the roots and stems are eaten in a similar way to celery stalks.

For centuries, angelica seeds and roots have been burned to fill homes throughout the European continent with its sweet fragrance. Oils from the plant flavor vermouth, and Chartreuse and Benedictine liqueurs.

Angelica's handsome stalks and showy flowers make dramatic additions to dried arrangements, while its leaves can be used as a fixative for potpourri. But angelica's most common use these days is as candied decorations on cakes and puddings. A caution should be noted here: angelica in any of its forms should never be used by anyone suffering from diabetes.

Work for Our Hands

Angelica Planting, Care and Upkeep

The herb gardener must be conscious of time when working with angelica. As July approaches, the seeds ripen and must be used immediately.

For such an adaptable plant, angelica seeds are remarkably short-lived. They need to be planted dir-ectly in the open ground as soon as they are ready, usually in July. Since angelica doesn't transplant well, this spot should be the plant's permanent home.

If you don't want to deal with sowing seeds, small containers of angelica are available from most nurseries. Plant in rich, slightly acid soil and water frequently, checking that the drainage remains good. It helps to cultivate around the base of the herb from time to time. Besides cutting back on weed growth, such cultivation improves air circulation to the roots.

If you wish to propagate by root cuttings or off-shoots, it's best to wait until midsummer of the second year to take the cuttings. Keep in mind that this herb requires partial shade to maintain both its distinctive flavor and its scent.

Harvesting angelica requires different methods from those used with most herbs, since this plant is a biennial. During the first year of growth, only side leaves should be picked. In the second year, the stalks may be harvested along with the leaves. Roots, too, can be dug during the midsummer months of the second year.

Once harvested, the stalks can be frozen or crystallized (candied) and the leaves dried. Yet it is generally agreed that all parts of the angelica plant are best when used fresh.

When this herb is allowed to flower in its second year, a substantial portion of its seeds will successfully self-grow, ensuring continuity. These seedlings, commonly called volunteers, will replace in full the second-year angelica you harvest.

Work for Our Hearts

The Need for Change

Not only does angelica number among the most adaptable plants, it also has created one of the most adaptable pests in the herb garden, the parsley worm. In midsummer, this green caterpillar with black stripes can be found attacking the angelica plant. But herbalists know better than to kill it. Within weeks, it will become a stunning black swallowtail butterfly, an endangered species on the North American continent.

The parsley worm offers us wonderful lessons about the need for adaptability and change in our lives. It has learned how to survive in its environment through mimicry. Over the centuries it has successfully adapted its shape and color to mirror the angelica plant. During this stage of its growth, it both feeds off this herb and uses it for protection from aggressors.

Later, when the angelica plant is ready to flower, the parsley worm reminds us that our lives are a series of becomings. For us to progress and live life to the fullest, we must embrace change as naturally as the butterfly does. We don't have to stagger from stage to stage in our spiritual growth. Rather we can view life as a process or journey along which we are guided by God.

Dostoevsky wrote that change is what people fear most, for we equate it with the unknown. Yet nothing is permanent in this life except change, leaving us two options: run from change or embrace it.

Spiritual growth embraces change. Although we may be uncertain about the future, we can be certain about God's active presence in our lives. We have not been left unprotected; nor are we at the mercy of a capricious, uncaring universe. We are loved and cared for by God. He wants to guide us through life's changes, so that we can emerge from transitions with new strength and understanding.

O God, grant us the serenity
to accept what cannot be changed,

*the courage to change what can be changed,
and the wisdom to know the difference.*

Reinhold Niebuhr

In the excercises that follow, we can honor the process of change in our own lives, using that adaptable herb angelica.

Exercise 1: Marking Major Transitions

Birthdays, weddings, baptisms and confirmations are only some of the joyous occasions which we celebrate by sharing a specially prepared cake. The art of cake decoration would be severely limited without the use of lovely green stems of candied angelica. To prepare this herb for any occasion requires us to follow these simple steps.

1. Cut a dozen young angelica stalks into three-inch long (8 cm) pieces. Wash and strip off the thin outer skin.

2. Soak overnight in a stainless-steel saucepan filled with water and one tablespoon each of salt and white vinegar.

3. Drain the angelica. Cover with water and simmer until the stems turn green. Drain once more.

4. Simmer the stems in a syrup made of 2 cups (450 g) sugar and 2 cups (1/2 litre) water for 30 minutes. Drain and refrigerate the angelica for three days. Don't forget to refrigerate the syrup also.

5. Place the angelica back into the syrup and simmer for 30 minutes once again. The syrup should candy the herb

this time, making the stems translucent and tender.

6. Place the angelica stems upright in a small, sterilized jar. Cover with the sugar syrup. Cap tightly and refrigerate until ready to use.

Exercise 2: An Angelic Nosegay

The first exercise for July helps us contribute to major life celebrations. This second exercise celebrates the more informal moments of change. Tussie-mussies, or nosegays, are presents we can give to friends who are moving into a new home, changing jobs, receiving promotions or ending courses of study with honors.

In years past, tussie-mussies were carried to help disguise the stench of urban streets and included herbs thought to prevent diseases. Later they became messages of love and caring. Today, with dried and fresh herbs and flowers, they are special handmade gifts from the heart for friends celebrating transitions in their lives.

1. Start with a few sprigs of flowering angelica. Surround them with a green-leafed herb. Tie the stems together with string or a twist-tie.

2. Keep placing successive layers of fragrant herbs and flowers around this angelica core, tying whenever necessary. Repeat until the tussie-mussie is the size you wish. Remember to vary the color and leaf shapes with each layer. End with a large-leafed herb, preferably angelica or soft lamb's ear.

3. Cut an X in the center of two large paper doilies, slip the

herb stems through and tie with a colorful wool yarn ribbon around the base. This gift is sure to please giver and receiver alike.

COMMON NAMES:
Lavender: English, Spanish, dwarf, French,
green French, spike.

BOTANICAL NAME: *Lavendula*

ORIGIN: Mediterranean

Lavender

The Abundant Herb

Lavender is the crown jewel of any herb garden. The four most popular varieties of this unusually attractive gray-leafed plant—English, Spanish, French and spike—prosper from hardy climates to the sub-tropics. Long a favorite with the public, lavender can be easily recognized by the ghostly beauty of its foliage and the delicate purple flowers bending on tall stems. Both the flowers and leaves have a wonderful aroma that enhances perfumes, sachets, potpourris and soaps. Lavender not only smells lovely but also looks stunning in fresh or dried floral arrangements. In any style of herb garden, this fragrant ornamental is guaranteed to add dramatic beauty.

A perennial shrub that grows no taller than three feet (90 cm) high, lavender has distinctive leaves that are thin-needled and downy. Equally delicate are its stems on which grow tubular, lilac-colored flowers in successive whorls. Lavender blooms from July through September, but the gardener must keep in mind that it takes two to three years before the seedling bears flowers in abundance. Lavender should be planted in well-drained, well-limed soil in a sunny, but sheltered, place.

Such was the freedom of God's will that no necessity could constrain him to the production of anything; such the bounty, that none could restrain him from the voluntary profusion of his goodness.

Walter Charleton, 1652

Owing to its beauty and abundance once it matures, lavender was widely appreciated by those living in ancient Mediterranean civilizations. Both the Greeks and Romans bathed in lavender-scented water. In fact, lavender's name came from the Latin word *lavo* meaning "to wash." This association continued through Tudor times when washerwomen were known as "lavenders."

Sometime after the fifth century, this herb unfortunately lost favor with the public, and religious authorities connected it with vanity, illicit sensual joys and mistrust. During the Renaissance its value was once again recognized, and lavender became an integral part of medicinal as well as ornamental herb gardens.

By the seventeenth century, lavender's greatest use was as an aromatic. Napoleon supposedly used sixty bottles of lavender water each month, pouring it over his body whenever he washed. Charles VI of France insisted that the royal cushions be stuffed with lavender, and Queen Victoria of England ordered that the wardrobes in the royal residences contain fresh and dried lavender.

Over the centuries lavender has been used to soothe

aching muscles and stiff joints by placing muslin bags filled with lavender leaves in the bath water. Oil from lavender flowers, when mixed with other herbs, makes a fragrant facial steam.

In the past, lavender was used in cooking and medicines. Distilled in water, lavender oil was given to cure migraines, fainting and stomach problems. Nowadays, lavender's use is confined mainly to cosmetics. Commercial operations in the United States and Europe cultivate lavender extensively to sell to the fragrance industry.

Work for Our Hands

Lavender Planting, Care and Upkeep
August is an incredibly lush month with herb gardens in full flower. No plant is more visually appealing than the long wands of flowering lavender moving en masse with even the slightest breeze.

On a hot August day, the fragrance of lavender permeates the garden, attracting bees as well as human visitors. Enjoying this month of bountiful lavender harvest is neither difficult nor time-consuming.

Lavender grows from slow-germinating seeds, root divisions or stem cuttings. The simplest and surest method to propagate lavender is to take cuttings from established plants in August and place them in sand. By late autumn, they will be rooted; by the following spring, they will be ready to plant in open ground.

One of the joys of caring for lavender plants comes

from the abundant ways this herb can be used. It looks good and grows well in formal and casual gardens. It can be trimmed back to preserve a sense of discipline and order or left to spread with abandon, crowded together in tall, glorious masses. Whether exuberantly informal or prim and proper, lavender fits into any garden design.

Perhaps it is best used to define central spots or fill open spaces in the garden. Its unique gray foliage keeps its color for most of the year, and lavender is one of the few herbs that looks good whether it is symmetrically shaped or left sprawling. Yet it does require periodic weeding, watering, pruning, trimming and harvesting if it is to survive season after season.

Besides well-draining soil, lavender needs protection from wintry winds. Planting it in a sheltered area solves this problem nicely. Trimming back mature plants works best in early spring, about the same time that the cuttings are ready for transplanting in their permanent home.

Harvesting lavender in late summer is the one chore that consumes a great deal of energy, considering the number of flowers picked. Since bees hover around this plant during the daylight hours, picking lavender is best done in late evening. Yet, for the brave and hardy, harvesting the stalks in midday yields the highest concentrations of oils.

The flowers are ready for picking when they show color but aren't fully open. The leaves have almost as much fragrance as the blossoms and even the seeds of this lovely plant are highly aromatic.

Work for Our Hearts

The Paradox of Abundance

Lavender grows with so much exuberance, it threatens to overwhelm the senses. Such abundance can be viewed as a blessing or a curse. We either love it or fear it.

Yet lavender reminds us that abundance exists in nature for a purpose that has nothing to do with our personal feelings of love or fear. No matter how rich, our natural resources are finite. They demand that we take proper care of the earth and all its creatures.

Our spiritual growth has always been tied to our stewardship of the land. We see this throughout the Bible, and also in Native American religious teachings. We were never given ownership over the world in which we live. We have been charged with being its caretakers. We are to strive for dominion, not domination.

When we experience lavender in all its August abundance, we know firsthand what proper use of the land can yield. We also realize that our efforts produce far more than we will ever use. Good stewardship involves caring as well as sharing.

On this fragile planet, not everyone is equally blessed with resources, opportunities or the means to meet the most basic needs. The true paradox of abundance is that it never touches all lives, even though the potential and challenge for it to do so exist.

The answer to resolving this paradox lies in the

spiritual realm. Good stewardship of all within our dominion creates an abundance we then can share with the less fortunate. Thus we learn to give of our possessions and ourselves.

We go beyond giving water to the thirsty; we teach them how to dig a well. We go beyond feeding the hungry; we teach them how to till the fields. We become managers of the earth, teachers of our fellow humans, and servants of God.

Humanity's impact on the planet has been grim. Statistics point to a future that is even worse. Our relationship to the earth and its resources has been catastrophic. Yet it isn't too late to build a new, spiritually based, relationship as caring and sharing stewards.

The lovely lavender reminds us that this world is a temple created by God, loved by God, and temporarily placed in our dominion. Our spiritual growth is directly connected with our role as managers of this temple.

If we properly do the job entrusted to us, we will help heal creation. If not, we will rupture our relationship with God and place the temple in even greater jeopardy.

Look to lavender during this month and answer the personal call to take care of the earth within our dominion and to share our abundance with others.

A Steward's Hymn

Creator Word, by whose great power
The oceans roar and plants do flower,
Create in us a love for Thee,
The Earth, all life, the sky, the sea.

O Word of God, who Earth did frame,
Who gives to us all things to name;
Grant us the knowledge of Thy ways
To care for Earth, to bring Thee praise.

Redeemer Lord who Earth did save,
Who lifted humankind from the grave;
Imbue us with redeeming grace
To heal the Earth, its blighted face.

Creator Word, by whose great power
The oceans roar and plants do flower,
May we, thine heirs, Thee emulate,
Our lives as stewards consecrate.

Calvin De Witt

Work for Our Lives

Caring and Sharing Abundance

Before we can go out to effect change in the world, we have to make stewardship a practical part of our everyday life. The spiritual discipline of caring begins with self and branches out from there.

Exercise 1: Caring

In this first exercise, we can learn to practice good management of our garden resources by following these six steps:

1. Water herb plants on a daily basis in early morning or late evening, a crucial task during the heat of August.

2. Continue to aerate the ground around each plant so that drainage remains good.

3. Check the leaves daily. When necessary, use natural pest repellents, available at most nurseries, to discourage attacks on the soon-to-be harvested leaves and flowers.

4. Weed at least once a week.

5. Take cuttings as you are harvesting the herbs. Place these cuttings in moist sand. Keep them in a shady spot as they begin to root. When the weather turns cool, they'll be ready to bring inside to enjoy throughout the winter.

6. Harvest and preserve your herbs, using the information provided in this book and others as a guide.

Exercise 2: Sharing

A terrific way to use lavender harvested from your garden is to make gifts called Lavender Wands to present to your friends and family. These are not only easy to prepare but also practical and long-lasting.

1. When the flowers closest to the top are just beginning

to open, gather fresh lavender spikes that have long stems. Use immediately.

2. Strip off any lower leaves and flowers.

3. Choose an uneven number of stems, preferably fifteen, seventeen or nineteen, and tie the stems together below the lowest flowers.

4. Gently bend the stems back evenly over the flowers.

5. Cut a five-foot (150 cm) satin or velvet ribbon and tuck one end of the ribbon into the blossoms.

6. Weave the ribbon in and out of the stems, using a basket weave, until the flowers are enclosed in the ribbon. A basket weave is simply bringing the ribbon over one stem and under the next.

7. When the blossoms are completely enclosed by the ribbon, wrap the ribbon around the stems and finish by adding a bow. You may want to tack the end with thread to keep it better secured.

8. Attach a notecard to each wand, stating how this fragrant present can be used in linen cupboards and among woolens, helping to capture the summertime aroma year-round.

COMMON NAMES:
Chicory, wild succory, blue sailors

BOTANICAL NAME: *Cichorium intybus*

ORIGIN: Europe

Chicory

The Timely Herb

An abundant roadside herb, chicory is a pretty, blue-flowered plant valued mostly for its taproot, which when roasted and ground adds flavor, color and bitterness to coffee. Its blossoms open and close with such regularity every morning and evening that Linnaeus included chicory in his famous floral clock, marking the hours with blooms. Even when cut for indoor displays, these bright blue flowers continue to open and close on time. Native to Europe where it is widely cultivated, chicory was introduced into the United States in the late 1800s. It has flourished across America ever since.

A hardy perennial, chicory is easy to recognize by its height, flowers, rootstock and milky juice. Standing five feet (150 cm) tall when fully grown, this herb has coarse-toothed leaves similar to dandelion leaves. A stiff, angular stem containing a bitter milky juice branches up to flowerheads that feature lovely blue rays. The chicory taproot is long and fleshy, light yellow on the outside and white inside. In fields and along highways, chicory can be seen flowering from July to September.

There is a time for everything, and a season for every purpose under heaven.

Ecclesiastes 3:1

Chicory long has held the nickname of "nature's timekeeper." For three months of every year, its blossoms mark the hour after sunrise and before sunset with amazing accuracy. Yet chicory has been used for more than late-summer timekeeping.

During the Middle Ages, its boiled leaves and flowers were wrapped in cloths and applied to painful inflammations and skin irritations. The juice of the leaves was recommended for treatment of jaundice and spleen problems, while the tea made from chicory flowers was used to release gallstones and eliminate digestive difficulties.

By the late sixteenth century, chicory was cultivated in the Netherlands, France, Belgium and Germany. Using cold-storage methods still popular today, the roots were forced indoors during the winter to produce leaves called *barbe de capucin* for French winter salad and crowns of *witloef* for Belgian salads.

Over the centuries, chicory roots have been boiled and eaten with butter. The entire plant has also been used as fodder or herbage crop for cattle in both Europe and North America.

During the early years of this century, chicory became a popular substitute for coffee in the southern United States. Even today, the city of New Orleans is known for its distinctive-tasting chicory brew.

Work for Our Hands

Chicory Planting, Care and Upkeep

Chicory is different from most herbs since it has two stages of development. The first produces the harvestable root, leaves and flowerheads. The second happens when you dig up the root, bring it indoors and bury it upright in damp sand to produce sprouts or heads of pale leaves.

Since chicory is so hardy and cold-resistant, it grows well under most conditions. Full sun, well-drained soil free from lumps that might split the root growth, and plenty of room to spread are all this herb requires to flourish.

Fertilizing needs to be done only twice during the growing season: before planting and again at mid-season. As with all herbs, the plants should be kept evenly moist. Within a hundred days, mature chicory roots will be evident.

If you won't be using the roots for salad or coffee, you may choose to produce the blanched heads in cold storage. Simply cut off the top two inches of the roots and pack them upright in a container filled with fine sand. Water them thoroughly and keep them in a basement where the temperature remains between sixty and seventy degrees Fahrenheit (15-20 degrees centigrade).

In three to four weeks, the heads will break the sand surface. When you harvest these by removing them with a sharp knife, you can use the roots again to force other harvests over the winter.

There are several warnings to remember about chicory. The leaves and heads should not be washed until you are ready to use them. You cannot freeze, can or dry any part of the plant and expect to retain the texture or taste. (The roots can be stored in a cool, damp place for several months. The leaves and sprouts stay fresh in a plastic bag up to one week.) Finally, always try to harvest chicory with the roots intact and avoid trimming the leaves.

Chicory is an unusual addition to the typical herb garden. Yet it brings with it many rewards for the patient gardener willing to invest the extra time and energy in producing successive harvests.

Work for Our Hearts

Trusting God's Timing
Of all the seasonal changes, autumn's approach is the most apparent. Summer's heat and lushness lingers for a seemingly brief moment each September before cool days and falling leaves greet us.

Autumn's entrance reminds us that time is a fragment of the infinite in a constant state of change.

Yet, at summer's end, when we see lovely chicory flowers blooming along the roadside, we realize something more about time. This herb, called nature's timekeeper, teaches us about trusting the timing of the Creator who created both time and eternity. If we linger to look and to think, we will discover hidden truths about the wisdom and ways of our God.

One of those truths was expressed by the unnamed author of Psalm 37. "Trust in the Lord and do good; dwell in the land and enjoy safe pasture," he wrote. "Commit your way to the Lord; trust in him and he will do this: He will make your righteousness shine like the dawn, the justice of your cause like the noonday sun."

Entering the autumn season, we come to see that underlying our busy days and hectic nights is a slower current. A holy movement that transcends daily life, it carries us far beyond human timekeeping, needs and concerns. It speaks of higher purposes, and it questions what we are doing with our lives.

We feel a mightier hand than ours at work, a hand we can learn to know better and trust. The seventeenth-century French cleric, François Fénelon, advised those seeking his counsel that "the best state to be in is that in which God's hand holds you; do not look beyond it, and think only of accepting everything from moment to moment." Sound advice for us to follow in this season of sudden change.

Each time we encounter chicory—this timely herb—we can practice the moment-to-moment acceptance called trust.

What you need to do is to put your will over completely into the hands of the Lord, surrendering to him the entire control of it. Say, "Yes, Lord, YES!" to everything and trust him so to work in you to will, as to bring your whole wishes and affections into conformity with his own sweet and lovable and most lovely will. It is wonderful what miracles God works in wills that are utterly surrendered to him. He turns hard things into easy, and bitter things into sweet. It is not that he puts easy things in the place of the hard, but he actually changes the hard thing into an easy one.

Hannah Whitall Smith

Work for Our Lives

Using Time Wisely

One way to use time to its fullest is to begin a regular pattern of meditation. There is no better place to communicate silently with our Creator than in an herb garden. Talking with God as we plant, weed and harvest our herbs is a natural, soul-satisfying activity. Creating a special meditation spot in which to be silent daily before the Lord is yet another.

Exercise 1: A Timely Garden Retreat

1. Choose a spot for a garden seat and build an arbor overhead. It need not be anything elaborate and can be done in any size herb garden. If you wish, you can plant roses and vines at the base of your arbor.

2. Purchase or create a sundial to match the informality or formality of your herb garden. Place it in full view of your

garden seat and surround it with chicory plantings.

Exercise 2: A Timely Treat

Looking inward through meditation is beneficial for our spiritual growth. So too is turning outward to others who are on similar life journeys. When we create room for communication with God in our lives, we also make room for communicating better with others. One way to facilitate this is to make and serve chicory as a coffee substitute or an addition to coffee when entertaining guests.

1. Take the roots from the first harvest, which is about 120 days after planting. Dig them up when the soil is dry and leave them on the ground for three to four hours.

2. Remove the tops, leaving about an inch of the crowns. Place in plastic bags with air holes. Store at 34 degrees Fahrenheit (1 degree centigrade) for no longer than three months in conditions that simulate those in a root cellar.

3. When ready to use, wash and dice the root.

4. Dry it thoroughly before roasting it in a moderate oven (350 degrees Fahrenheit; 175 degrees centigrade) on a baking sheet.

5. Grind the diced, roasted pieces and use as you would coffee beans.

6. Serve with sweet rolls and enjoy both this chicory drink and the company.

COMMON NAMES:
Winter savory, savory, bean herb

BOTANICAL NAME: *Satureia montana*

ORIGIN: Mediterranean, Southern Europe

Winter Savory

The Zesty Herb

The name **winter savory** fits this dainty, lacy herb well. Easy to grow and attractive, winter savory is a low bushy evergreen that thrives even in the sandiest soil. Although it is closely related to summer savory, this winter variety differs in three important ways. It's hardier, it's a perennial and its leaves are more aromatic.

As its name suggests, this herb adds spice to almost any food and is an effective salt substitute too. Most commonly used as a culinary herb, winter savory stimulates the appetite while adding its unique hot and peppery flavor to a wide range of ethnic dishes. Bees find savory's abundant flowers attractive and can be found hovering among them late into October.

Winter savory grows ten to fourteen inches (25-35 cm) high yet fills out so nicely that it is frequently used as mainstays in traditional herb and rock gardens alike. Winter savory is noted for its small, stiff, needle-shaped leaves and square stems, which become woody as they develop. In contrast to the sharp-flavored leaves are the delicate white or purple flowers that bloom profusely well into autumn. When taken indoors, winter savory continues to grow with typical zeal. As if to prove its uniqueness, winter savory becomes fire retardant when well-watered.

I ask you, Lord,
to develop in me
an immeasurable urge towards you,
an affection that is unbounded,
a longing that is unrestrained,
a fervor that throws discretion to the winds!

Richard Rolle

Both the Greeks and the Romans appreciated winter savory. While the Greeks used it in highly spiced sauces poured over fish and poultry, the Romans flavored vinegar with it for use in dressings.

Pliny the Elder, Roman scholar and author, planted winter savory near his bees to improve the taste of their honey. Hippocrates valued this herb for its medicinal properties.

Ancient Druids used savory in their rituals, and the Elizabethan herbalist Nicholas Culpepper recommended it to treat deafness and bee stings. "Mercury claims dominion over savory," he advised. "Keep it dry by you all the year, if you love yourself and your ease."

Known to the present day in Germany as the "bean herb," winter savory is valued for the pungent taste it adds to all bean dishes. Yet a tea made from winter savory leaves remains a popular drink for those suffering from stomach and intestinal disorders. It can also be used as a gargle for a sore throat.

Winter savory is grown commercially throughout the world since its leaves are an important flavoring ingredient in salami and seasoning mixes. Whether winter savory is used fresh, dried or frozen, its popularity with cooks worldwide has not diminished.

Work for Our Hands

Winter Savory Planting, Upkeep and Care

Winter savory is simple to grow if you remember that it prefers soil that is sandy, relatively moist and well drained. It has no serious pest or disease problems, but it requires full sun to thrive.

Although seeds can be planted in open, well-fertilized ground two to three weeks after the late spring frost, using cuttings nurtured indoors during the winter will give your herb garden an early start.

Winter savory can also be propagated by layering. During the summer choose a healthy branch growing close to the ground, and cut a notch in it. Cover three to four inches (8-10 cm) of the notched stem with three to four inches (8-10 cm) of soil. Bend the growing tip vertically above the ground and support it with a stake. Within six weeks, roots will form at the notched spot. At that point, you can cut the buried stem from the savory bush and transplant it.

The plant's growth slows with age so that winter savory needs replacing every four to five years. It does fine when left outside, so long as the temperature doesn't drop below 10 degrees Fahrenheit (-12 degrees centigrade). A careful trimming every spring is the only other requirement for this herb.

To harvest, you can pick the fresh savory leaves and stems throughout the growing season. Due to its hardiness, two harvests each year are usually possible. To dry, cut off the top six to eight inches (15-20 cm) of the plants as soon as they start to flower.

If you prefer fresh winter savory, place your garden plants in containers each October and bring them into a protected area of your home to winter. They'll continue their enthusiastic growth in the months ahead.

Work for Our Hearts

Maintaining Zest for Spiritual Growth

During this month of blazing autumn colors, the winter savory burns with a flavorful intensity that rivals the colorful October world. Its pungent taste, second harvest and abundant autumn growth affirm the cycle of life, death and rebirth.

Savory reminds us that autumn need not be a melancholy time; it provides lessons in zestful living. Ralph Waldo Emerson wrote that nothing great was ever achieved without enthusiasm. To grow is to live with zest and rise to great truths with enthusiasm.

Like fire, spiritual growth burns within us and demands both constant feeding and watching.

Shedding light on truth isn't enough. Our growth must also spread warmth to all who come in contact with us.

A life lived fully becomes a life in which concern for others outweighs concern for ourselves. We are energized when the focus shifts away from self and toward others. When this happens, we have grown in maturity and our days become filled with an energizing joy.

As we enter this season of harvest, winter savory's prolific flowers are constant reminders to celebrate and share the bounty. Spiritual growth, like physical growth, cannot take place in a vacuum.

As we mature inwardly, our relationships will begin to reflect that maturity. We shed light and create warmth.

Spiritual growth, by necessity, is painful. But with abundant zest, we can make it less burdensome and more satisfying. In the process, we can savor anew the colorful creation that is October.

My whole heart I lay upon the altar of thy praise, a whole burnt-offering of praise I offer to thee. Let the flame of thy love set on fire my whole heart, let nought in me be left to myself, but may I wholly burn towards thee, wholly be on fire towards thee, wholly love thee, as though set on fire by thee.

Augustine

Work for Our Lives

Zestful Exercises

Rather than mourn the end of the harvest, you can make October a time of joyous, practical planning as you prepare your indoor gardens. With six easy steps, you can transfer your enthusiasm for herb gardening indoors.

Exercise 1: The October Indoor Garden

1. Choose which herbs you wish to grow indoors over the winter. Culinary herbs are the most practical and popular, particularly winter savory, the mints, oregano, French tarragon and basil.

2. Pot root divisions of your healthiest outdoor plants after the last harvest, making sure that sprouts appear on top. Four-inch (10 cm) pots work best for this purpose.

3. Build trays filled with pebbles and place the potted herbs in them.

4. Find windows with a southern exposure and let the herbs winter in the trays there. They need about five hours of light per day.

5. Feed the herbs every two weeks with a well-balanced plant food.

6. Water the plants with tap water that is at room temperature, and make certain that the herbs are kept away from drafts and extremes in temperatures.

Following these guidelines, you will savor the fragrance and greenery of herbs throughout the year.

Exercise 2: Savory Vinegar

A second way to enjoy winter savory throughout the year is to create herb vinegars for gifts and daily culinary use.

1. Pick young, leafy sprigs of winter savory and basil right before the plants flower. Wash and dry them carefully.

2. Place the leaves in a marble mortar and crush with a pestle. You should end up with 1/2 cup winter savory leaves and 1/3 cup basil leaves.

3. Crush three garlic cloves and mix in with leaves.

4. In a saucepan, heat one quart (one litre) of red wine vinegar until it is close to boiling. Place the herb mixture in a clean jar, pour the vinegar over the herbs and cap the jar tightly with a non-metallic lid.

5. Let the mixture steep for three weeks.

6. Strain the vinegar through a cheesecloth into an attractive gift container. Insert a fresh sprig of winter savory, close with a cork stopper, seal with red sealing wax and store at room temperature.

7. Accompany your winter savory vinegar gift with a favorite recipe in which it can be used. Attach a bow to the recipe and tie it around the neck of the vinegar bottle.

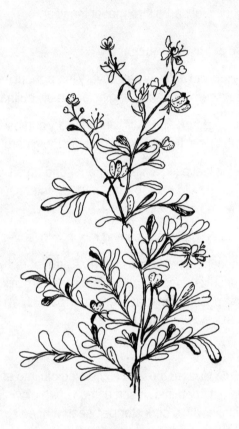

COMMON NAMES: Rue, herb o' grace

BOTANICAL NAME: *Ruta graveolens*

ORIGIN: Southern Europe

Rue

The Herb of Grace

This striking plant with its charming yellow star-shaped flowers and blue-green foliage graces the herb garden well into winter. Once popular as a medicinal herb, rue is used almost exclusively now as an ornamental.

Rue's long and varied history remains part of our language. The word rue conveys penance, pity or forgiveness, thus giving rise to this plant's common name, herb o' grace. Its lacy leaves and erect stance make rue an attractive garden filler, one that well deserves its botanical name *ruta,* which means "to set free" in Greek. Because of its association with freedom, rue has been declared the national plant of Lithuania.

A hardy perennial that thrives in full sun and slightly acid soil, rue bears its lovely flowers from early June to late September. Yellow blossoms cover the entire plant, giving it a bushy appearance. Growing nearly three feet (90 cm) tall, rue is a semi-evergreen that also produces interesting seed pods. Its green leaves are unusually bitter tasting and give off a musky aroma that repels garden pests. This herb is often placed next to rose bushes to deter Japanese beetles.

Grace is the gift of God which is only given to us to draw us on to God himself.

Bede Jarrett

Rue has one of the richest traditions of any herb in use today. Centuries before Shakespeare employed rue's emblems in **Hamlet** and **Richard II**, people in many cultures had already come to "rue the day."

According to legend, the gods gave Ulysses this herb to free him from Circe. Over time, rue became a standard defense against witchcraft. Chinese emperors as well as Greek and Roman leaders learned from bitter experience to take small doses of rue to make themselves immune to assassination attempts through food poisoning. (In large doses, rue itself can be poisonous.)

Priests in the early Roman Catholic Church began using sprigs of rue to sprinkle holy water at High Mass. By the Middle Ages, the belief arose that rue tea freed people from a whole list of complaints ranging from hysteria and snake bites to poor circulation and old age. Bunches of rue were used to ward off plagues, fever, headaches and household insects.

Rue became a popular herb to plant around stables in order to repel flies, and the Chinese used it similarly to discourage mosquitoes. Interestingly enough, rue leaves are recommended by Chinese herbalists today to fight malaria.

Perhaps the most unusual stories concerning rue come from Greek folktales. In them can be found the secret to growing rue successfully: steal young plants from an unwitting neighbor. The flavor from stolen plants, they advised, was always more pungent and the antidote for poison more effective.

In this century, rue has been used as an insect and moth deterrent, as a garden ornamental and in dyes. Since some people who come in contact with this herb react with an allergic rash, every part of the plant needs to be treated with caution.

Work for Our Hands

Rue Planting, Upkeep and Care

Rue seeds germinate easily in two weeks at moderate temperatures. In early spring, after the last frost, the seeds can be planted in rows 15-18 inches (40-45 cm) apart. Since rue doesn't compete well with weeds, the seedlings should be cared for conscientiously.

Late spring is an ideal time to divide established plants. Take root cuttings only after the blooms fade from bushier plants.

Throughout the summer, branches for floral arrangements can be picked. The blue-green foliage, either fresh or dried, makes an attractive addition to any arrangement.

If you allow the seed pods to dry on the branches, remember to harvest some of them before they open. These seeds can then be used the next spring for planting, while the dried, opened seed pods can be used for decorations.

Dried rue leaves can be made into an ointment to

treat rheumatic pains, sprains and muscle strains. Rue should never be used during pregnancy, and large doses may be poisonous.

One of the more colorful ways to use your rue harvest is to produce a rosy red dye from the roots. After six years or more, the rue plant tends to get woody; this is an excellent time to gather the roots and replant the area with healthy younger rue.

Rue has no serious pest or disease problems. It can be container-grown as an annual, and it also winters nicely in a protected area when surrounded with mulch.

Work for Our Hearts

Grace-Filled Language

Rue's lore is not limited to legends and outdated beliefs. For centuries, rue has played an important role in the intriguing language of florigraphy. In the unspoken messages of herbs and flowers, rue's bitter leaves convey repentance while its lovely blossoms speak of grace.

We could not ask for a better lesson during this month of winter preparations. As the darkness lengthens each November night, we grow increasingly aware of the gift of light. Our thoughts turn naturally to the change of heart that reflects the change of seasons.

It is no coincidence that Ambrose Bierce called November "the eleventh twelfth of a weariness." Nor is it surprising that Americans celebrate Thanksgiving each year during this very month. In November, repentance and grace intertwine.

If repentance is God's voice admonishing us to change, grace is his constant loving mercy towards us. Through God's grace we have salvation.

Repentance is the leavetaking and last look backward to a lifestyle that is over. Grace is the seed of a new life, one firmly embedded in faith and trust. Together they prepare us for the possibilities ahead.

Rue thrives with both leaves and flowers intact. In our lives, grace and repentance can coexist with as much beauty and strength.

Within us, repentance doesn't need to be labeled "failure" but rather indicates a growing determination to change for the better. Rather than accept self-loathing, we reach up to God in love.

Grace, on the other hand, is always a gift. In some mysterious way, we learn to express outwardly the new inner harmony and balance granted us. We stop self-regarding and begin God-regarding instead.

During the shortened days of November, we can look to the rue wintering in our herb gardens and trust that the seeds of new life exist even now. And when we examine our indoor rue harvest, we remind ourselves again that our lives depend on the grace of God.

Take, Lord, and receive all my liberty, my memory, my understanding and my entire will, all that I have and possess. Thou hast given it all to me. To thee, O Lord, I return it. All is thine; dispose of it wholly

according to thy will. Give me thy love and thy grace,
for this is sufficient for me.

Ignatius of Loyola

Work for Our Lives

Coded Herbal Messages

In the Middle East, Turks sent one another herbal greetings conveying verses of classical poetry. The Chinese and Japanese conducted affairs of state using the specific language of flowers. By the 1700s, this coded speech came to England, reaching its romantic peak in the Victorian era.

For gift-giving herb gardeners, florigraphy is a wonderful way to send a caring message on any occasion. Here is a short list you may want to consult when putting together a bouquet of dried or fresh herbs. Explaining this new language to the bouquet recipient will only add to the mutual enjoyment of gift-giving.

Herb	Message
Rue leaves	*Repentance*
Rue flowers	*Grace*
Rosemary	*Remembrance*
Lemon Balm	*Sympathy*
Horehound	*Health*

Herb	Message
Mint	Virtue
Sage	Esteem
Parsley	Celebration
Camomile	Patience
Thyme	Courage

Exercise: A Graceful Centerpiece

Dried arrangements are ideally suited for November weather and gift-giving. They require no care, travel easily and are colorful additions to almost any home or office.

The key to creating a graceful arrangement is harmony between the dried herbs and the container. Delicate bunches of tiny daisies and baby's breath look wonderful in miniature containers not usually associated with bouquets—a copper candlestick, a chunk of coral, an antique pewter inkwell.

On the other hand, when you have great armfuls of herb branches, you might consider using something more substantial. A butter churn, copper boiler or wooden chest make delightful containers.

Almost any household object can be converted into a holder for dried arrangements. Just remember to keep your thinking flexible and your mind open to the possibilities of mixing and matching herb flowers, leaves and seed pods with various containers normally used for other purposes.

Once the container and herbs are chosen, attention can then be paid to establishing harmony in form, color and texture. Don't be afraid to experiment, mixing light with dark foliage, sophisticated blossoms with rough pods, and delicate flowers with wild herb branches. Harmonious relationships arise from the unexpected.

Artful arranging is no less than the creation of a still life mirroring nature. A truly graceful centerpiece exudes the beauty of this harmony above all else.

COMMON NAMES:
Sweet, garden and knotted marjoram,
marjoram, joy-of-the-mountain

BOTANICAL NAME: *Marjorana hortensis*

ORIGIN: Mediterranean and western Asia

Marjoram

The Joyful Herb

This bushy, compact shrub certainly deserves the name marjoram, which means "joy of the mountain." Perhaps no herb is so widely appreciated or so versatile. Cultivated throughout the world from ancient times to the present, marjoram has been used as an effective medicine, tasty food and sweet perfume.

Its sprightly appearance matches its name as well. With its delicate, fuzzy leaves and small white flowers, which look like tiny knots, marjoram adds cheeriness to any setting. Since the whole plant is highly aromatic, this herb makes its presence known to all our senses.

A tender branching perennial, marjoram usually is grown as an annual since it doesn't winter well in most climates. Standing no taller than eighteen inches (45 cm) when fully grown, this herb is often confused with oregano (wild marjoram). Although both belong to the same family, marjoram isn't as hardy or as strong tasting as oregano. Neither cold nor drought-resistant, marjoram needs frequent watering and full sun when brought indoors for the winter. When treated with such care, marjoram will blossom with clusters of fragrant flowers throughout December.

True joy is the treasure of the soul, and therefore should be laid in a safe place, and nothing in this world is safe to place it in.

John Donne

Throughout the East, marjoram became a symbol for joyous love and respect. Considered a sacred herb in India, marjoram was also honored in ancient Egypt, Greece and Rome. Venus, the Roman goddess of cultivated fields and gardens, reputedly was the first to grow this herb. The Greek goddess Aphrodite associated its use with both valor and joy.

In the Middle Ages, marjoram became "the scrub-woman's helper" since it was widely used as a strewing herb, to scent wash water and to clean furniture. Its association with joy—or at least merriment—also continued. Before the discovery of hops, marjoram leaves were an important ingredient in beer making. Additionally, marjoram tea was effective in relieving indigestion and hangovers.

By Elizabethan times, the English were hearing Shakespeare compare marjoram to a virtuous gentle-woman, the Italians were adding its zesty flavor to sauces, the French were using it as a cold remedy and the Germans were preserving sausage with it.

Over the next two centuries, marjoram served a number of purposes. Dried and ground, it became popular as snuff. The flower tops were used in dyes for wool and linen. In the culinary world, the classic seasoning *bouquet garni* incorporated marjoram as a necessary component.

Today we value marjoram more in cooking than in medicine. It is frequently added to meat dishes, vegetables and milk-based desserts. Unfortunately, oil of marjoram now is limited to occasional use in herbal soaps, shampoos and perfumes.

Work for Our Hands

Marjoram Planting, Upkeep and Care

Marjoram is a strangely vulnerable plant. Although it tolerates light shade and poor soil, it needs good drainage, much water and a frost-free climate to survive.

In one respect, marjoram can provide a delightful surprise for the gardener because it self-sows easily. When the earth is warm in the spring, the pot of marjoram that went to seed indoors over the winter need only be taken outdoors and replanted.

The soil should be fertilized before planting, not after. Too-rich soil will produce an abundance of leaves with little flavor. To foster growth, the branches need to be trimmed back.

When the first blooms appear, the leaves can be harvested by cutting along the branches several inches. On indoor plants particularly, fresh leaves can be picked several times during the winter season.

The key to preserving marjoram flower tops and leaves is to dry them quickly, crumble them and store in dark, airtight containers. Although marjoram leaves can be frozen, they lose some of their flavor this way.

With these efforts, marjoram will continue to supply culinary needs throughout the year and make joy-of-the-mountain a staple in the herb gardener's kitchen.

Work for Our Hearts

The Many Facets of Joy
Joy has as many facets as marjoram in the different seasons of its development. There is the quiet expectancy of its dormant stage, the simple pleasure of new growth, the boisterous good cheer of full bloom, and the satisfaction and celebration of the harvest.

In our spiritual lives, we enter and exit similar stages more than once. Joy comes to mean something greater than elation. It is a permanent gladness of heart or, as Eric Bentley wrote, "bliss without otherworldliness." We feel it throughout the year in its different guises, and we acknowledge it as the result of living life intensely and well.

Too often we equate joy with material goods and creature comforts. We tend to ignore Thomas Jefferson's wise words that joy is "neither wealth nor splendor, but tranquility and occupation."

The marjoram plant can teach us much about living with intensity yet tranquility, occupied with work and leisure that we engage in fully and well. This joyful little herb gives daily lessons in the need for versatility and strength, tenderness and purpose. It reminds us to give of ourselves and serve others, to heal and bring pleasure. It even plays a small part in helping us to learn more about balancing the earth's energy, water and temperature levels.

Marjoram blossoming on the windowsill in winter seems a more fitting symbol of the Christmas season than the traditional evergreen trees and holly boughs. It speaks of birth in the midst of darkness and the satisfaction that comes with approaching all that we face each day with good intent and integrity.

Joy, like marjoram, is a wholehearted affair. It has less to do with what happens to us and more to do with our attitude toward each happening. If we are ready to experience life to the fullest—to serve to the fullest and to love to the fullest—we know joy. We rarely have time to question whether or not we are happy. We are too busy living in the present moment.

Through the changing seasons, joy-of-the-mountain unfolds, sharing its benefits with others. When we permit ourselves to unfold all the spiritual powers planted within us, the result is much the same.

In this month of too-short days and heightened holiday demands, joy can become the steadfast core of our existence. We need only look beyond self to others, beyond our wants to others' needs. Some of the greatest exclamations of joy can be found in the Psalms in the Bible. Psalm 98, for example, shows the depth of joy the Psalmist feels in pronouncing God's greatness.

Sing for joy to the Lord, all the earth;
praise him with songs and shouts of joy!
Sing praises to the Lord with harps;
play music on the harps!
With trumpets and horns,
shout for joy before the Lord, the king!

Roar, sea, and all creatures in you;
sing, earth, and all who live there!
Clap your hands, oceans;
hills, sing together with joy before the Lord,
because he comes to rule the earth!
He will rule all peoples of the world
with justice and fairness.

From **Psalm 98**

Although joy connects us with goodness and God, its roots require firm planting in the events and relationships of daily living. As the calendar year draws to a close, may we all know the healthy flowering of such joy in our lives.

Why should we go to heaven weeping, as if we were like to fall down through the earth for sorrow? If God were dead, we might have cause to look like dead folks; but "the Lord liveth, and blessed be the Rock of our salvation." None have the right to joy but we; for joy is sown for us, and an ill summer or harvest will not spoil the crop.

Samuel Rutherford

Work for Our Lives

Joyful Living

Gift giving traditionally marks the Christmas holiday season. For gardeners, making our herb harvests "gift worthy" is simply a matter of customizing.

Exercise 1: *Bouquet Garni*

Don't let the name intimidate you. Creating a gift of this classic seasoning can be a joyful experience. Traditionally, **bouquet garni** is a "broth posy." Three common herbs are tied together in a little bundle, then added to stews, soups or sauces. It is retrieved from the dish before serving.

To make the broth posy, cut a four-inch (10 cm) square of muslin or cheesecloth and fill it with the following ingredients.

1. For beef-based dishes, combine one teaspoon each of dried marjoram, basil and parsley.

2. For poultry dishes, combine one teaspoon each of dried tarragon, summer savory and lemon balm.

3. For milk-based dishes, combine one teaspoon each of dried marjoram, thyme and rosemary.

Don't forget to attach a long thread to the bundle so it can be removed easily when the dish is ready to be served. It is a thoughtful gesture toward your guests to attach recipe cards listing the dishes the **bouquet garni** flavors best.

Exercise 2: A Living *Bouquet Garni*

A special selection of live plants is another way to tailor your garden gifts to a particular friend's culinary needs. Find an interesting wicker basket or hamper and fill it with a selection of herb plants used in preparing *bouquet garni*.

Have fun repotting the plants with unusual, colorful or offbeat containers or tubs. You might even want to plant some of the herbs together if it meets their growing requirements and shows them off to advantage. And, as always, don't forget to add recipe cards for making various *bouquet garni*-flavored foods.

Exercise 3: An Herbarium

For those friends newly interested in herb gardening, an herbarium—a collection of dried, labeled herbs—is a much appreciated gift. Photo albums make the best booklets for preserving and recording herb information, and they can be found readily in most stores.

Devote one page to each herb. Begin by placing specimens of pressed flowers, stems and leaves beneath the transparent self-adhesive plastic sheeting. To this you can add decorative cards identifying the herb by name, place of origin, uses and other data of interest.

Be sure to leave some of the pages blank so that your friends can add to the herbariums as their own collections grow. You can make each book as elegant or as simple as you wish. Knowing your friends' tastes, you can develop sections of special interest to them.

For a Shakespeare fan, you can choose herbs popular in an Elizabethan garden: marjoram, parsley, savory, lavender and rue. For a bread-maker, you might consider herbs commonly used in breads—chervil, dill, chives, parsley, anise and garlic. For a biblical scholar, herbs mentioned in the Bible could be the central themes: anise, hyssop, cumin, mint, basil, bay leaves and coriander.

December calls for celebrating new life, centered around Christ's birth. In this season of simple beginnings, no more appropriate reflection of heartfelt sharing could be offered than gifts from the herb garden. As the holidays approach, sit back, review your harvest and discover the number of different ways you can transform your herbs into gifts that give real joy.